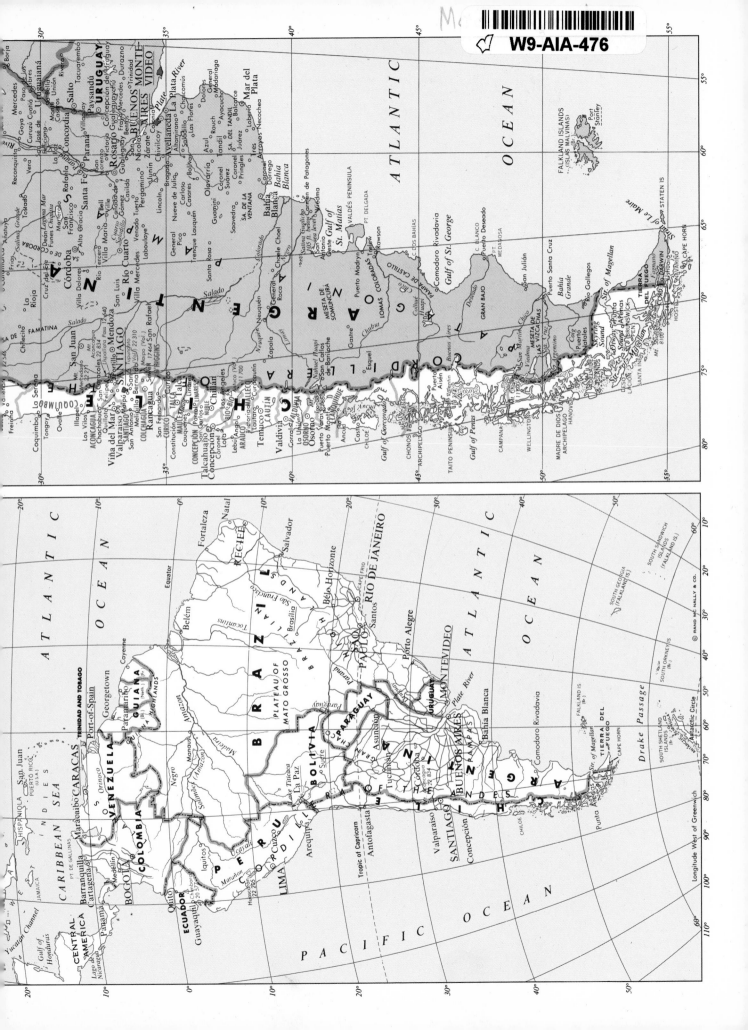

LIFE WORLD LIBRARY

THE ANDEAN REPUBLICS

TIME
LIFE
BOOKS

LIFE World Library
LIFE Nature Library
LIFE Science Library
The LIFE History of the United States
Great Ages of Man
LIFE Pictorial Atlas of the World
The Epic of Man
The Wonders of Life on Earth
The World We Live In
The World's Great Religions
The LIFE Book of Christmas
LIFE's Picture History of Western Man
The LIFE Treasury of American Folklore
America's Arts and Skills
300 Years of American Painting
The Second World War
LIFE's Picture History of World War II
Picture Cook Book
LIFE Guide to Paris
TIME Reading Program

LIFE WORLD LIBRARY

THE ANDEAN REPUBLICS

BOLIVIA, CHILE, ECUADOR, PERU

by William Weber Johnson
and The Editors of LIFE

TIME INCORPORATED   NEW YORK

COVER: Two derby-hatted
Indian women who live
in the highlands of the Andes
carefully coax a llama
up a hillside near the shore
of 12,500-foot-high Lake Titicaca.

ABOUT THE WRITER

William Weber Johnson first became interested in Latin America through ex-
tensive travel in Mexico while on vacation from college. After receiving a bache-
lor's degree from DePauw University and a master's degree from the University
of Illinois, he became a staff writer and correspondent for Time Inc. and filed
stories from Central America and the Caribbean. He was a combat correspondent
during World War II, and subsequently returned to Latin America as chief of
the TIME-LIFE Bureaus in Mexico City and Buenos Aires. While in the latter
post he became acquainted with the Andean nations, to which he returned for
an extended trip while preparing the text of the present volume. Mr. Johnson
has written many articles on Latin America, particularly Mexico, and on the
American Southwest for a number of national magazines. Now a professor
of journalism at the University of California at Los Angeles, he is the author of
the LIFE World Library volume *Mexico* as well as of a children's history of the
conquistadors, *Captain Cortés Conquers Mexico,* and a biography of Harold
Osman Kelly, a primitive painter from Texas.

Contents

TIME-LIFE BOOKS

EDITOR
Norman P. Ross
TEXT DIRECTOR   ART DIRECTOR
William Jay Gold   Edward A. Hamilton
CHIEF OF RESEARCH
Beatrice T. Dobie
Assistant Text Director: Jerry Korn
Assistant Art Director: Arnold Holeywell
Assistant Chief of Research: Monica O. Horne

•

PUBLISHER
Rhett Austell
General Manager: Joseph C. Hazen Jr.
Business Manager: John D. McSweeney
Circulation Manager: Joan D. Manley

LIFE MAGAZINE

EDITOR: Edward K. Thompson
MANAGING EDITOR: George P. Hunt
PUBLISHER: Jerome S. Hardy

LIFE WORLD LIBRARY

SERIES EDITOR: Oliver E. Allen
Editorial Staff for *The Andean Republics:*
Assistant Editor: David S. Thomson
Designer: Ben Schultz
Chief Researcher: Grace Brynolson
Researchers: Jill Adams, Edward Brash, Lea Guyer, Evelyn
Hauptman, Donald Newton, Louise Samuels, Ellen Youngblood

EDITORIAL PRODUCTION
Color Director: Robert L. Young
Art Assistant: John M. Woods
Picture Researchers: Margaret K. Goldsmith, Barbara Sullivan
Copy Staff: Marian Gordon Goldman, Patricia Miller,
Dolores A. Littles

The text for the chapters of this book was written by William Weber
Johnson; the picture essays were written by Harvey Loomis and Da-
vid S. Thomson. Many of the photographs were taken by Cornell
Capa. Valuable help was also provided by the following individuals
and departments of Time Incorporated: Dmitri Kessel, LIFE staff pho-
tographer; Doris O'Neil, Chief of the LIFE Picture Library; Content
Peckham, Chief of the Time Inc. Bureau of Editorial Reference; and
Richard M. Clurman, Chief of the TIME-LIFE News Service.

Introduction

Latin America is embarked on a great undertaking: to achieve its modernization, not at the cost of freedom, but through a vast expansion of freedom. The popular faith in this purpose is so profound and so pervasive that the late President John F. Kennedy by affirming it as an underlying premise of the Alliance for Progress won a place in the Latin American temple of fame reserved for the continent's most cherished heroes—Bolívar, Martí and San Martín.

There are those who contend that this grand aspiration contains a fatal flaw: that rapid economic development is incompatible with social improvement. Yet, whatever the impact of rapid economic advance will be, the overwhelming fact of contemporary Latin American history is that a fossilized social structure is crumbling before what a Latin American statesman has characterized as a "final assault in the age-old battle for the equality of all men."

Nowhere in Latin America is the ferment for social progress more evident than in the Andean countries covered in this book. Chile's Christian Democratic Party, which came to power in 1964 on the promise of "revolution with freedom," has since won an absolute majority in the Chamber of Deputies. It has an unprecedented opportunity to extend the benefits of democracy, which have heretofore been reserved for the privileged, to all the people of the nation.

Bolivia, whose revolution of 1952 forever separated it from a feudal past, may have suffered a setback in 1964 through a military coup. But, as the writer of this book observes, "the forces for change set in motion by the revolution will almost certainly continue to move inexorably toward the ultimate goal—rehabilitation of the long-repressed Indian population and development of the nation's economy."

Peru's Government, led by the Acción Popular party, is committed to a "revolutionary reform of national structures." It inherited this purpose from an older party, the APRA, which is still a powerful force in the country. It seems inevitable, with these parties on the scene, that the large Indian population is destined to be given genuine citizenship and to be incorporated at last into Peruvian society.

In Ecuador the pressures for change are still diffused. That they exist with great force, however, is unquestionable; organization and articulation are bound to emerge and channel these pressures into a powerful social and political force.

It is the particular merit of this excellent and readable book that it captures the accents of the changes sweeping the Andean countries. The men, the movements and the aspirations that are transforming these countries are presented with exceptional skill. And, as is perhaps always the case, when change is understood the past is seen in fresh perspective, and culture and even geography become alive.

The readers of this book will discover the vitality of a newly emerging civilization. The Spanish conquest produced a tricolored spectrum of humanity in the Andes—white, mestizo and Indian—and a confrontation of indigenous and Western cultures that if often fruitful was also productive of injustice. The Spaniards used the color spectrum to impose a rigid social scale and employed the differences of culture as an instrument of subordination. But where conquest and empire divided, freedom has increasingly served to unite. First came independence; then a growing belief in ideals of social justice. Now the business at hand is to create modern, democratic nations. All these movements have served to break down the old Spanish racial and cultural stratifications. In the end, if freedom is preserved, neither the white man nor the mestizo nor the Indian will triumph—rather, it will be a triumph for humanity.

BEN S. STEPHANSKY
former U.S. Ambassador to Bolivia

High in the bleak, wind-swept Bolivian highlands, three Indian women arrange their wares at dawn in the marketplace of Laja, a small

town near La Paz. The church is of characteristic Spanish design.

1

The Mountain World

IN the Andean world, time, climate, landscape and humanity are telescoped and intermixed in a mosaic that is magnificent, confusing, charming and awesome. The four Andean nations—Peru, Ecuador, Bolivia and Chile—encompass regions of eternal snow and tropical rain forests, of torrential rivers and deserts where rain never falls, of volcanic fire and glacial ice, of tundra and tropical lagoons. There are orchids, spices and sharp-spined cactuses, monstrous reptiles, 163 different kinds of hummingbirds, people who still live in the Bronze Age, people who live in great luxury and people who live in places where people have no business living at all.

In the jungles of eastern Peru and Ecuador, there are savages who hunt with poison-tipped arrows and shrink human heads. But the teatime crowd in the Rotunda of the Gran Bolívar Hotel in Lima is very like the teatime crowd in New York's Plaza, London's Savoy or the Ritz of Paris—finely gowned women, men who know the intricacies of international banking and, of course, some thin-blooded descendants of the lands' original conquerors. Not far away from this elegant crowd, there are descendants of the *victims* of the conquistadors. Some of them are abject and mute. Others are bitter and resentful: Indian men who reclaim ancestral lands with muskets and machetes, and Indian women who carry dynamite in their shawls and still revere an ancient fertility goddess. There are sweet-smelling suburbs, bright with bougainvillaeas, geraniums and roses, and there are appallingly filthy and noisome slums. The great and lovely churches of Quito and Cuzco are filled with pious people, gold leaf, and relics of saints and conquerors; and once a week Bolivian Indians celebrate a sort of Black Mass on the heights overlooking La Paz.

IN their various aspects the Andean countries may remind one of Libya, Tibet, Norway, Switzerland, Iowa or the steppes of Russia. The faces of the people may reflect kinship with soldiers from Spain's province of Estremadura, scholars from the ancient University of Salamanca, Irish adventurers, Arab peddlers, English railroad builders, Jewish refugees, Oriental contract laborers, American sailors, African slaves, Basque shepherds, German burghers, Scottish bankers, Slav farmers, Albanian fishermen, Italian vintners and, of course, Indians, who were there before any of the others came. In the cities the language is Spanish. On the beach at the Peruvian seaside resort of Ancón or on the ski slopes of Portillo in Chile it may alternate with English, French, German or Italian. In the highlands the Indians' language will be either Quechua or Aymara, and only occasionally Spanish. But the people who live on one of the many tributaries of the Amazon will know neither Spanish nor Quechua nor Aymara, but will speak Campa, Aguaruna, Cashibo, Machiguenga or another jungle language that is spoken nowhere in the world but in their village.

It is a region in which the imagined clink of gold and the illusory scent of cinnamon have led men to stupendous feats of exploration and discovery. The Spaniards found here a people with seemingly inexhaustible supplies of gold and silver, and mines that promised more, so that in the 16th Century world the ultimate in wealth was described as *vale un Perú*, "it's worth a Peru." But it is still a land inadequately explored, not entirely discovered;

still a land of mystery that inspires fanciful notions. It has been held that the Creation according to Genesis took place in eastern Bolivia, that Peru was the Biblical Ophir, that Solomon's ark was made of Amazonian hardwoods, that the country was originally settled by Noah's great-grandson.

There are many legends of lost cities. Some Chileans still believe that hidden away in the southern Andes is a "City of the Caesars," a place where the buildings have walls of gold and silver. In 1911 Hiram Bingham, the American historian-explorer (and later U.S. Senator), found the grand and ghostly "lost" city of the Incas on the crest of a mountain known as Machu Picchu. How many more such cities lie hidden by jungle growth or forgotten in the towering mountains no one knows.

It is a region of earthquakes, avalanches, droughts and floods. The geological forces that thrust up the mountains locked great wealth in gold, silver, copper, iron, tin, oil and nitrates in the earth. The same forces also made it difficult if not impossible for man to get at these riches—and almost equally difficult to pursue such humble, useful tasks as building a road or a school. The area's most familiar aspect is one of hostility to man and his orderly, sensible progress. In Peru, Ecuador, Bolivia and Chile the flora and fauna and, of course, the magnificent scenery have been made by mountains. The mountains also have shaped domestic politics, interregional prejudices, foreign policies, economics, folkways and the character of the people. Differences of race, heritage and outlook are strengthened and sustained by the mountains.

THE Andes form part of a chain of mountains that runs the length of the Western Hemisphere, from Alaska to Cape Horn, but it is in South America that the peaks reach their spectacular climax, second only in height to the Himalayas. Here they rise out of the tropical waters of the Caribbean and march southward for more than 4,000 miles before sinking again into the frigid sea at the southern tip of the continent. They spread out into separate cordilleras—strings of mountains—occasionally separated by fertile valleys but more often by high, cold tablelands. The cordilleras are sometimes crossed by separate, transverse chains, the junctions forming tumbled mountain masses known as *nudos,* or knots. In tiny Ecuador alone, there are more than a dozen peaks exceeding 15,000 feet in height. The country's highest peak is Chimborazo, which rises 20,577 feet. South of Ecuador, there are even higher ones: Peru's Huascarán, 22,205 feet; Tocorpuri, on the border between Bolivia and Chile, 22,162 feet; Ojos del Salado, which rises between Chile and Argentina, 22,550 feet. Highest in the entire system is Aconcagua, 22,835 feet, which is also near the Argentine-Chilean frontier. These peaks are taller than the greatest mountain in North America (McKinley: 20,270), in Europe (Elbrus: 18,356) or in Africa (Kilimanjaro: 19,565). Only the mountains of Asia are higher.

In between the towering peaks stretch virtually unbroken chains of high, rocky mountains. At some places in Chile the system narrows to a width of only 20 miles, and in Bolivia it reaches its greatest breadth, almost 400 miles. Most passes are higher than 12,000 feet, and many of the bleak, barren intermontane plateaus are at even greater height—14,000 feet in Bolivia, for instance. Many of the approaches to the mountains are abrupt, in some places the altitude increasing two miles in a horizontal distance of 15. The distance from the summit of Aconcagua, which is more than four miles above sea level, to the offshore bottom of the Peru-Chile Trench is nine miles, the world's longest descent from great altitude to great depth.

Between the mountains and the sea is a shelf of land which extends for most of the length of the South American continent. Approximately half of this shelf—all of the Peruvian coast and the northern part of Chile—is a desert. The cold, northbound Humboldt Current produces a temperate climate in what would otherwise be tropical latitudes, but it also robs the west wind of all moisture before it reaches land. The Andes themselves shut off the

HOW INDIANS ADAPT TO ALTITUDE

At an altitude of 10,000 feet most people begin to suffer from lack of oxygen. The Andean Indian, who lives at altitudes up to 17,000 feet, has developed certain physical characteristics to get the most use of what oxygen exists at those heights. His lungs are bigger than normal, so that he inhales more air with each breath. In the walls of every person's lungs, there are tiny sacs in which oxygen is transferred from the air to the blood; in the Indian's lungs these sacs are permanently dilated to provide maximum surface for the oxygen transfer. The circulatory system is also modified: the Indian has about two quarts more blood than do lowlanders, and the red blood corpuscles, which carry the oxygen, are considerably bigger. Finally the heart itself, which pumps blood and oxygen throughout the body, is larger than normal by almost 20 per cent.

moisture-bearing trade winds from the east. So dry is this desert that mummies 9,000 years old have been preserved in the sands of Paracas in Peru, as have brilliantly colored textiles woven some 2,500 years ago. Here and there westward-flowing streams from the mountains trickle down into the desert. Where they do, there are luxuriant oases, for the sands of the desert are fertile where watered, producing crops of cotton, sugar cane and rice in the north, and grain and fruit in the south.

At irregular intervals a tropical current called El Niño, "The Child," flows down from the north and drifts over the cold Humboldt Current. Then the rain pours down; dry river beds turn into torrents; people, houses and crops are swept into the ocean. The rich marine life of the Humboldt Current is either destroyed or driven away, and the fishing industries come to a halt. The sea birds, source of guano fertilizer, either migrate or starve. Afterward the desert blooms like the tropical region it would be if it were not for the Humboldt Current.

The contrast between the coastal desert and the highlands is no greater than that between the Andes and the tropical country on the eastern side of the mountains. Great quantities of rain fall on these eastern Andean slopes. Here there are streams, clear as crystal at first, which rapidly become fast-flowing rivers, brick red to chocolate brown in color. East of the mountains they spread out and become the headwaters of the mighty Amazon.

The rivers cut deep chasms in the mountains and drop quickly from the forested mountain slopes to the vast river-basin jungle that makes up at least half the national territory of Ecuador, Peru and Bolivia. It is a region rich in hardwoods, natural rubber, wild fruits and vegetables, spices, and plants which form the basis for many pharmaceuticals and drugs. But, however rich, the region is so inaccessible that it is sparsely inhabited, and trading centers, such as the Peruvian towns of Iquitos and Pucallpa, are rare. There are some enterprising missionaries, such as those of the Maryknoll order and the Summer Institute of Linguistics, a few selfless practitioners of tropical medicine, a few adventurers, traders, dreamers and fugitives from justice, the last usually whiskered and rum-sodden. The rest are primitive people, living in ways little changed in a thousand years—men who hunt monkeys and toucans for food and pound out telegraphic messages on hollow logs, and women, bare to the waist, who deliberately deform their children's heads and work spidery patterns on textiles and ceramics.

BETWEEN these two extremes of the Andean world—the coast and the jungle—lies the part most characteristic of the whole: the highlands, the mountains, and the intermontane valleys and plateaus, variously known as the *páramos*, the *mesetas*, the *punas* and the *altiplanos*. It is one of the world's highest inhabited regions, rivaled only by Tibet. A number of the important cities are above average human altitude tolerance. Quito, the Ecuadorian capital, lies at more than 9,000 feet. Cuzco, the heart of the Inca Empire, is at 11,000. In Bolivia, La Paz is at 12,000. And the mining centers of Cerro de Pasco in Peru and Potosí in Bolivia are both above 13,000. The air is thin, and the night cold is intense. Nevertheless a majority of the mid-Andean population lives in the highlands. Bolivian Indian miners work at altitudes up to 17,000 feet (and after work may play a fast game of soccer for recreation). Some Bolivian sportsmen ski at Chacaltaya, far beyond the level at which lowlanders require the help of tank oxygen.

The altitudes have developed a specialized type of physique. The highland Indians' chests are deep and broad, to take in more of the thin air. Their hearts and blood volume are both one fifth larger than normal, and their pulses are slower. Arms and legs are short, hands and feet small, thus reducing the distance that the heart has to pump the blood and also reducing the area exposed to the cold. Natives of the Andes can walk barefoot in the snow with no apparent discomfort. For nonnatives, there is a very real threat of *soroche,* or altitude sickness, which may be marked by nausea, dizziness, indigestion,

nosebleed, blackouts, even heart attacks. People acclimated to the altitude are sometimes uncomfortable when they descend to sea level, and highland Indians are very susceptible to lowland diseases. The Inca rulers decreed that for health reasons highlanders should never be required to go to the lowlands and vice versa—a ruling which the Spanish Crown and the Spanish Viceroys wisely copied.

When the Argentine José de San Martín marched his army up through Andean passes to liberate Chile in 1817, both men and mules suffered from *soroche.* The soldiers ate garlic to relieve it and rubbed garlic on the teeth and gums of their mules. A more current bit of folk medicine is that layers of newspaper worn under one's clothes will help prevent altitude sickness. Highland Indians perform astounding feats of endurance at high altitudes, carrying tremendous loads, working in fields or mines from dawn to dark. But they stave off fatigue, hunger and thirst by chewing wads of dry leaves of coca, a native plant which is the source of cocaine, mixing the leaves with lime to activate the numbing effect. Distended cheeks on pre-Inca portrait jugs indicate that addiction to coca has been going on for a long time. Non-coca-chewers at high altitudes wisely avoid any needless exertion. When hotel and restaurant workers went on strike in La Paz recently, they did not walk a picket line, but hired trucks and rode back and forth in front of the struck establishments.

THE Indians of the highlands are separated from the rest of the world by the physical barriers of the mountains and the equally formidable barriers of language, ignorance and poverty. They are an agricultural people by heritage and instinct, but the agricultural resources are meager, and their lives are, more often than not, lived in misery and hunger. Crops are largely limited to potatoes (an Andean native which is both cultivated and found growing wild, some species being no larger than a marble), sweet potatoes, a few other edible tubers, maize, quinoa (a native grain) and beans. Cows, sheep and goats are grazed in the lower valleys, but the poor pasture of the mountainsides and high plateaus will support only the llama, a camel-like animal of great utility, and its cousins, the alpaca, the guanaco and the vicuña.

Although it is slow and contrary and will carry no more than 100 pounds, the llama is used as a beast of burden. It provides wool (the alpaca and the vicuña produce a higher-grade wool) and is a source of tallow, leather and meat. Its droppings are gathered for fuel. The llama is even used for sacrifice and soothsaying. Dried llama embryos are sold in Indian markets; they are buried under the doorstep of a new house for good luck, or in a field to insure fertility. Only the Tibetan yak, which can be saddled and milked, exceeds the llama in versatility. The llama is suspicious of all strange humans, particularly white ones, and it may spit, bite or kick. Or it may lie down with its load and groan.

USABLE land is even more limited than are the crops. Highland Indian farmers in the centuries since the Spanish conquest have been compressed into smaller and smaller areas. Some Indians today own no more than a single furrow of land. Others are completely landless and indentured to large landowners, working as sharecroppers or for wages that may range from eight to 15 cents a day for three or four days a week in exchange for the use of a stony, sterile acre for subsistence crops.

Chileans joke about the "crazy geography" of their country; one of their gifted writers, Benjamín Subercaseaux, wrote a book about Chile with that phrase as its title. It is a freakishly shaped nation, 2,600 miles long and in no place wider than 250 miles—and in most places much narrower. But in one sense Chile's geography is more rational than that of its sister republics in the Andean world. For all of Chile—and all Chileans—are on one side of the Andean wall of stone and ice, united by the mountains instead of divided as the others are. Peru, Bolivia and Ecuador are sharply cleft by the Andes, each section alienated from the others by the physical barriers and by the wide differences in altitude, economy and human attitudes.

Such regional differences have long divided Ecuador. Guayaquil, the country's commercial center and principal seaport, is brisk and progressive despite the tropical climate. It is politically liberal and has little in common with and almost no sympathy for Quito, the old, conservative and mountain-bound capital.

In Bolivia most of the population is concentrated in the Altiplano, the high, bleak southwestern corner of the country. But the fastest-growing part of Bolivia is in the east. People in the Santa Cruz area, center of both an agricultural and an oil boom, have in the past talked of secession and are more neighborly with Brazil and Argentina than they are with their own countrymen from the highlands.

Iquitos, the capital of Peru's vast jungle area in the east, is similarly closer to Brazil in terms of commerce and human behavior than it is to Peru. By airplane Iquitos is little more than 600 miles from Lima, Peru's political capital. But until there was air service the surest way to get from Iquitos to Lima was to go 2,300 miles down the Amazon to the coast, up through the Atlantic and Caribbean, across Panama, then down the Pacific coast to Callao, Lima's port—a total of some 7,000 miles.

The Oriente territory, which lies on the far side of the Andes, is so remote and inaccessible from the remainder of Ecuador that large sections of it have been yielded to neighboring countries: Brazil, Colombia and particularly Peru.

The difficulties of commerce in such a fragmented world have resulted in various affronts to national pride. The fine hats woven by Ecuadorians from *toquilla* fiber had for many years no easy access to the outside world. They were shipped to Panama for marketing and are consequently known around the world as Panama hats. The rich nut of the *Bertholletia excelsa* is abundant in northern Bolivia, but because it could be more easily exported by way of Brazil it became known in world markets as the Brazil nut.

THE solution to much of the economic and political disunity lies in roads, and each of the countries today is making valiant efforts at road building. Peru's President, Fernando Belaúnde Terry, is vigorously pushing plans for an international highway along the eastern margins of the Andes which would link those regions of his own country with those of Ecuador and Bolivia; it would eventually be connected with lateral highways in the individual countries, running through the Andes toward the Pacific coast. It would also, in time, link up with Brazil's road system, so that someday there would be a transcontinental network of roads. But the problems are staggering. In the mountains, if roads can be built at all, they must be carved from solid rock. In the coastal lowlands, there is no rock for ballast, and the route is soon lost in mud or sand. Roads must go through deserts, thick jungles and over chasms, where bridges must be built at dizzy heights.

IN the past three decades the airplane has done much to reduce isolation and bring the disjointed segments of this disparate world together. Ancient two-engine planes circle up and dodge between Andean peaks, crew and passengers sucking on oxygen tubes. The national Air Forces are clearing landing strips and offering freight and passenger service where no commercial service would be feasible. Missionary planes, such as those of the Jungle Aviation and Radio Service, operated under the direction of U.S. missionaries, regularly visit Indians who have never seen a wheeled vehicle.

The transistor radio is also helping to bring the peoples of the Andean world together. In many Indian market towns the sight of a traditionally dressed Indian with one ear glued to a tiny, hand-held radio is becoming common. Through the radio many of the Indians have for the first time become conscious of their nationality and aware that they are, at least by law, citizens of a democracy and entitled to its benefits.

Making democracy function is a problem that has beset each of the Andean countries at one time or another. All have had trouble finding constitutions that work. Peru has had 12, Bolivia 14, and Ecuador has had 16 and is working on a 17th. Chile, rather more stable than the others, has had seven, but only two in the last 132 years. Coups d'état, dictatorships and government by military junta have been a way of life.

Peru suffered a military coup as late as 1962, and Ecuador in 1963. Dissolution of the old, trouble-causing Army was one of the first acts of the revolutionary Government that took over Bolivia in 1952. Then, characteristically, the new Army created by the revolutionary regime ousted the duly elected civilian President in November 1964. Chile alone among the Andean countries has been free from military domination for many years. The armed forces

became facts of national life in each of the four countries partly because of endless disputes over boundaries. Although each one helped the others in the struggle to throw off Spanish rule, such unity was short-lived, and they have been quarreling over their boundaries ever since independence.

Boundary problems date back to the conquest. Spanish geography was vague and casual. There are at least six different names in Spanish records for the island of Puná, now part of Ecuador, and four for the city of Sucre in Bolivia. Measurements were more approximate than precise, so that land descriptions tended to be confusing. Uncertainty as to the dividing lines between areas controlled by the various Spanish conquerors led to civil wars among these old comrades in arms. For many years the northernmost boundary of Chile was marked only by a whalebone stuck in the sand. Peru began disputing its boundary with Ecuador almost as soon as the latter won its independence in 1830. Discovery of nitrates in the Atacama Desert brought on the War of the Pacific in 1879 between Chile on the one hand and Peru and Bolivia on the other, with victorious Chile taking territory from each country and robbing Bolivia of its corridor to the sea. Bolivia has, in the years since, lost territory to Brazil and Paraguay, while Ecuador has been reduced by cessions to Brazil, Colombia and Peru. As late as 1941 Peru sent an invading army into Ecuador in a boundary dispute. Ecuador still insists that its boundaries reach far beyond where Peruvian maps put them.

THE many difficulties of the Andean countries —the national and regional jealousies, the internal fragmentation, political instability and social inequality—seem all the more strange in view of the fact that most of the area was once ruled well by a single Government—that of the remarkable Incas. At its peak the Inca realm covered most of the present-day Andean republics, from the northern boundary of Ecuador to central Chile. The Inca Empire was remarkable not only for its size but also for its achievements in the arts, agriculture, engineering and the techniques of government. The evolution from the old sense of order, efficiency and justice to today's divisiveness and unrest is the story of the Andean world.

On an island of reeds floating in Lake Titicaca Indian women and children learn to read. Their woven boats are unique to the lake.

A Hardy People in a Harsh, Monumental Land

On the high tablelands which lie among the rugged peaks of Ecuador, Peru and Bolivia, there live some six million Indians whose hardy existence has seen little change for thousands of years. In their Andean world the scenery is breathtaking, but life is difficult. As stern, uncompromising masters, the dominating mountains cast the Indian's life in a harsh mold. The soil is poor, affording him only a meager subsistence; the climate is hostile and the air is thin. But the Indian, poor and uneducated, is infinitely enduring. Short, wiry and phlegmatic, he matches the mountains with a stoic determination all his own.

VILLAGE SCENE in Tiahuanaco in western Bolivia contrasts the brooding, massive face of an ancient stone statue with the animated figures and bright dresses of Indian market women.

VAST LANDSCAPE of Bolivia's highlands dwarfs an Indian herdsman, his llama and his flock of sheep. The thatched huts in the distance look as Indian huts have looked for centuries.

FILE OF INDIANS hauling farm produce to market on their backs (*above*) plods along a trail near a group of farm buildings in western Bolivia. The difficulty of farming the thin Andean soil is increased by the steepness of the hillsides.

MOTHER AND CHILD, who have come in from the country to spend Sunday in the Peruvian mountain town of Chincheros, stand by a wall (*left*) dating back to Inca times. The woman carries her baby in a wool shawl slung across her back.

COLORFUL HAT, of a design traditional in the Cuzco region of Peru, adorns a woman at market day in Chincheros. She is drinking *chicha*, a native beer usually made from fermented corn, although almost any other vegetable will do.

AN INLAND SEA, 12,500-foot-high Lake Titicaca stretches away below two Indian herdsmen and their llamas. The world's highest lake navigable by steamships, and South America's second largest, 138-mile-long Titicaca lies between Peru and Bolivia.

A VAST PLATEAU in the Peruvian Andes is etched by a winding stream and by the railroad which runs between the highland towns of Puno and Arequipa. There are few roads or rail lines in the Andes, which is a chief reason for the area's poverty.

A JUMBLE OF CRAGS which are part of Bolivia's rugged Cordillera Real overshadows Cochabamba, the country's second-largest city (pop.: 92,000). Cochabamba is Bolivia's tourist center and is at one end of a modern highway, completed in 1954, which constituted the first vital link between the highlands and the city of Santa Cruz in Bolivia's underpopulated interior.

Supervised by a "mayordomo" with whip in hand (at right), a work squad of Indian women in the Ecuadorian highlands sorts the tiny

potatoes that are basic to the Andean diet.

RAISING DUST on a dirt road in Peru *(left)*, a truck carries Indian highlanders to work on a hacienda in the valley, where the land is fertile.

BREATHING FIRE, the peak of Villarica in southern Chile glows in the twilight. It is one of the most active of Chile's dozen volcanoes.

23

2

The Ancient Sense of Order

THE cold wind of the highlands raised the ear flaps of the old man's knitted cap and made the tattered fringes of his poncho dance in the morning sun. His sandaled feet shuffled through the bunch grass. He struck the frosty ground sharply with the tip of his *vara,* the silver-decorated staff that identified him as an official of a highland Indian community.

He was followed by seven small boys. They were young, but they were nearing the completion of as much education as they would ever have. They had learned to be obedient to their elders, to distrust outsiders, to plant and harvest potatoes and quinoa, to care for sheep and llamas, to be respectful to Christian saints and to fear pagan spirits, such as the Aukis that live in the mountains and the Ccoa that sends hailstones to destroy the crops.

Now they were being taught the boundaries of the *comunidad.* As the old man walked the boundary line he spoke of land disputes, some with white *hacendados,* or large landowners, and some with other Indian communities. Some disagreements had been mild, some bloody. Some had been in recent years, some a century before, but they were described with equal immediacy.

When the old man reached the final *mojón,* the pile of stones marking the boundary, he squatted on the ground. The eldest boy was told to lift the top stone of the pile. Under it he found, just as the old man said he should, two crossed twigs and a quid of coca leaves left from the last time the old man had walked the boundaries. This indicated that no one had tampered with the marker, that no effort had been made to move it and cheat the community of its precious land.

Having finished his lecture, the old man made the boys stand. With his *vara* he gave each of them three stinging blows on the backside so that they would not forget what he had told them. The simple, rude ceremony—together with many other folkways—is a link between today's Andean Indians and the great Inca civilization of their forefathers.

THE language spoken by the old Indian was Quechua, which the conquering Incas used as a universal language among the various peoples brought together under their rule. Today it is spoken by some six million Indians in the four Andean republics, and it gives them a greater unity than does loyalty to their individual countries. The laws and decrees of the nations of which they are, technically at least, citizens are remote and in many cases utterly incomprehensible.

Another link with the past is the concern for the *comunidad*, the Indian community, an entity more important than either the individual or the nation. The community is the lineal descendant of the *ayllu*, or family-community group, whose antecedents stretch back into dim prehistory, even antedating the Inca Empire. The Incas used the *ayllu* as a basic unit in their elaborate sociopolitical structure. The community, then and now, operates on a basis of cooperative effort, and often the land is communally owned and used. Preservation of the ancient boundaries against encroachment—whether by the white man or another Indian community—is a matter of great common concern. It often leads to distrust, or *desconfianza*, a characteristic Indian attitude directed at all outsiders, even if they are only census takers or dispensers of free medical services.

A final link with ancient times is the almost mystical attachment to the land. The whole history of the Andean peoples, before and after the Incas, has been one of conquering a difficult and often inhospitable earth and making it fruitful. The cycle of clearing,

planting and harvesting became the basis of a carefully observed calendar, and the calendar provided a framework for government, laws and even religion. The sun, which made the crops grow, was the kindliest element in a cold, difficult, mountainous world. The hour of noon, when the sun was directly overhead and cast no shadows, came to be the holiest hour of the 24. The solstices were times of fear— fear lest the sun forsake the earth. The sun was worshiped as a god and was believed to be the father of the Inca, or ruler.

That an entire civilization came to be called Inca —a term which correctly described only the emperor —is a curious historical inaccuracy, but no other term for these remarkable people has ever been devised. Why this confusion came about is one of many puzzles in a little-known past—a past which was as baffling to the Inca peoples themselves as it was to become to Spanish chroniclers and later historians and students.

In the 16th Century, Garcilaso Inca de la Vega, the son of a Spanish soldier and an Inca Princess, tried to unravel his people's past. In his narrative, *The Royal Commentaries*, he quotes an old Inca general: "'. . . at one time, all the land you see about you was nothing but mountains and desolate cliffs. The people lived like wild beasts, with neither order nor religion, neither villages nor houses, neither fields nor clothing, for they had no knowledge of either wool or cotton. Brought together haphazardly in groups of two and three, they lived in grottoes and caves and, like the wild game, fed upon grass and roots, wild fruits, and even human flesh. They covered their nakedness with the bark and leaves of trees, or with the skins of animals. Some of them even went unclothed. And as for women, they possessed none who were recognized as their very own.'"

THE old general's description, although certainly based on folk tales, may have been accurate as far as it went. Seven thousand or more years ago a group of very primitive men lived on the shores of the Pacific Ocean near what is now the luxurious Peruvian summer resort of Ancón. They were probably descendants of a people who had migrated across the Bering Strait from Asia in the even more remote past and had begun to populate the American continents. There were also early settlements in the Peruvian highlands. By 500 B.C. these highlanders had become skilled stone carvers, potters and temple builders, inspired by visions of a god with feline features and monstrous fangs. Somewhat later other cultures developed closer to the coast. The people on the arid peninsula of Paracas in southern Peru had wondrous skills in spinning and weaving, and they produced textiles that were masterpieces in texture and design. Others, such as the Moche people to the north, became highly sophisticated sculptors and painters. The Chimu people, also of the northern Peruvian coast, were great city builders, as can be seen at the vast ruins of Chanchan, near Trujillo, Peru.

But the greatest advances were to be made by the highland peoples, first by those of Tiahuanaco, just south of Lake Titicaca, and by the Wari people, who came from near the Ayacucho region, and later by the Incas. The civilization of the Incas was the last in a series of great cultures, as was that of the Aztecs in Mexico; because the Inca civilization was the predominant one when the white man came to the New World, more is known about it than about any of the others.

Why a great civilization should flourish in the Andean highlands, or why, for that matter, man ever settled there at all, is hard to understand. It is a region in which there are, occasionally, fertile valleys with an agreeable climate. But more characteristic are lofty mountains, yawning chasms, fast-flowing and unnavigable rivers, and broad, cheerless, windswept plateaus, sparse vegetation, bitterly cold nights and air so thin that the average person has great difficulty breathing. Some investigators believe that the predecessors of the Incas may have been forced to settle in this inhospitable region by warlike tribes in the lowlands. They may have chosen it because of a racial memory of the Mongolian highlands of Asia. They may have settled the area because they found the potato growing there, which offered the kind of basic, storable food crop that is a prerequisite for the development of any stable culture. Or it may be, as some theorizers have conjectured, that in those forgotten times the climate was more benign because the Andes were not as high as they now are.

FAR-REACHING EMPIRE of the Incas expanded dramatically under a succession of remarkable rulers. Driving both north and south from the empire's nucleus in the region of Cuzco, these rulers conquered most of the Andean world. They knit together their domain with a system of roads stretching some 5,000 miles from the empire's northern to its southern limits.

Whatever may have been the reason for settlement in such an unlikely place, the Incas had legends of precursor peoples—a race of giants, a race of desert dwellers, a race of warriors and so on, running back into the past for 5,000 years or so. But the Incas dated their existence as a separate and distinct people from Manco Capac, the first great Inca, or ruler, of whom their legends took account. Manco Capac was, according to these legends, the son of the sun, and he had emerged, accompanied by his sister, Mama Ocllo, from the waters of Lake Titicaca about 1200 A.D. Mama Ocllo, the legend continued, had become Manco Capac's wife, thus establishing a pattern of sanctioned royal incest which continued through much of the Inca dynasty.

Of the first seven Incas after Manco Capac—Sinchi Roca, Lloque Yupanqui, Mayta Capac, Capac Yupanqui, Inca Roca, Yahuar Huacac and Viracocha Inca—little is known. There were wars with tribes in the vicinity of Cuzco and campaigns of conquest down to the shores of Lake Titicaca. In the light of what was to happen this amounted to little more than skirmishing. For more than two centuries the Inca realm was a small one, changing in size and shape with the fortunes of war and bearing little resemblance to the mighty empire that was to follow.

USING A "QUIPU," a string counting device, an Inca official keeps track of stored food. This drawing and the one opposite are from a 17th Century chronicle of Peru.

But in 1438, less than a century before the Spaniards broke up the empire, one of the greatest of the Inca rulers came to the throne in Cuzco. He was Pachacuti Inca Yupanqui. He and his son Topa Inca Yupanqui, who succeeded him in 1471 and ruled until 1493, were probably the two greatest rulers of aboriginal America. As conquerors they rank with Philip and Alexander. As organizers they had no equal in the ancient world.

Pachacuti began by subduing all his neighbors in the Cuzco area and then moved up the Urubamba valley to the north. Later he swung west, conquering as he went, and finally south as far as the southern shore of Lake Titicaca. He sent his brother Capac Yupanqui on an expedition into northern Peru. Capac, in pursuit of some deserters from his army, went even farther than Pachacuti had ordered and conquered the rich province of Cajamarca. Such was the absolute authority of the ruling Inca that when the brother returned, victorious, he was executed by Pachacuti for exceeding his orders. Pachacuti carried out a few more campaigns but then busied himself consolidating the empire and converting Cuzco into an imperial capital.

His young son, Topa Inca, who was destined to be his heir (although there were elder sons), carried on the conquest. Topa made the long march to Ecuador, conquered the fierce Cañari Indians, converted them into devoted followers and with their help overcame the Quitu nation, strongest in Ecuador. He marched to the Ecuadorian coast, subdued the towns of Manta and Huancavilca, and, according to legend, made an expedition to some Pacific islands—possibly the Galápagos but probably islands closer to the mainland. Returning, he marched against the Chimu nation on the north coast of Peru.

The Chimu people, well established and prosperous, had all their fortifications facing south, where the Incas were supposed to be. Topa attacked from the north and gained an easy victory. He pushed his conquests along the coast to what is now southern Peru, then crossed the Andes and descended into the eastern lowlands to subdue tribes in the Amazon basin.

This expedition was interrupted by an uprising of a conquered tribe in the Lake Titicaca region. Topa marched there at top speed, fought fierce battles on both the north and the south shores of the lake, and extended the boundaries of the empire into the central highlands of Bolivia. Then, in what must have been a march of almost unbelievable difficulty, he swung through mountains and across deserts into what is now Chile and pushed the tough, warlike Araucanians south as far as the Río Maule. This became the southern limit of the Inca Empire. With the exception of one more minor excursion into the eastern forest region he devoted the rest of his rule to consolidation and organization. His son Huayna Capac was later to push the empire's northern limits as far as the present-day boundary between Ecuador and Colombia, but the major portions of the realm had been put together by Pachacuti and Topa.

It was an empire that covered 380,000 square miles, equal in area to the Atlantic states of the U.S. Its population was probably about eight million, although some estimates have ranged as high as 16 million. The speed with which it had been together and the firmness with which it was held together are amazing. Even more remarkable were its sociopolitical nature and the apparatus invented to coordinate the empire and make it function.

There were a number of prime problems. One was —just as it is today—a shortage of arable land to produce food for a large population. It was a country of high plateaus where few plants could survive, of jungle land where exuberant tropical growth choked out crops, of mountain slopes too steep for cultivation and of bone-dry deserts. There was little game, and there were few domesticated animals, notably the llama and the guinea pig.

Another problem was the difficulty of communication and transportation over an almost impossible terrain. Still another was diversity of religion. The Incas worshiped a creator god named Viracocha, and a number of lesser gods, of which the most important was the sun. The Aymara, whom the Incas subjugated, were said to worship caves, streams and stones. Indian tribes on the Pacific Coast understandably regarded the sea as a god.

INSPECTING A BRIDGE, an official surveys one of the Incas' rope spans. The drawing is by Felipe Guamán Poma de Ayala, whose book has much Inca lore.

And there was, of course, diversity of language.

The governmental system which evolved under the Incas to cope with all these difficulties was a despotism reinforced by a caste-based society. But, strangely, the despotism was combined with a benign form of state socialism, in many respects more daring— and successful—than that of any contemporary socialist state.

Part of the land was reserved to the sun god for the support of temples and the priesthood, and part to the Inca. The rest was shared by the people and was farmed communally. Once a year the land was reallotted, each family getting enough for its current needs.

Fixed portions of the crops went to the state and to the state religion. Able-bodied men also had to contribute their services as soldiers or as workers on public projects such as road building. The land of the old, the sick and those absent on military duty was farmed by others in the community. Surpluses in one area were distributed in areas where crops were poor or were saved for a less bountiful year. Fleece sheared from the llamas and alpacas went into Government storehouses and was distributed equitably to the women for spinning and weaving (but vicuña wool, one of the finest in the world, was reserved for the Inca ruler and the nobles).

To increase the land's productivity, guano was brought from the offshore islands of Peru and used as fertilizer. Whole mountainsides were terraced with stone walls; fertile soil was collected and carried up the mountains to enrich the planting areas. Since the terraces were built on steep slopes, the difference in altitudes enabled the Incas to produce a variety of foodstuffs. Elaborate systems of ditches and sluices brought water to the terraces. Many of these remarkable terraces are still in use today. In desert regions vast aqueducts brought water from the mountains, as much as 400 miles away, to form rich, productive oases.

To solve communication problems and to speed troop movements the Incas built a network of roads which can be compared with the famed road system of the Romans—and the Incas constructed theirs over far more difficult terrain. Although the wheel was unknown many of the Inca roads were wide enough to compare favorably with today's highways. Roads through the desert were walled in to protect them from drifting sand. Roads up the mountains switched back and forth to reduce the grade and then in the steepest parts became stone stairways. One road followed the coast from Tumbes, near the Ecuadorian frontier, to Talca, in Chile, a distance of more than 2,000 miles. Another, in the highlands, ran from Quito to Cuzco, around Lake Titicaca, through parts of Bolivia and Argentina, and down into Chile, some 3,000 miles. In places the coastal and mountain highways were joined by lateral roads. Fast-flowing rivers and chasms were crossed by suspension bridges made of thick vegetable-fiber cables (renewed once a year) which supported swaying wooden walkways. Some such bridges were still in use as late as the 19th Century; an account of one of them supplied the key element in Thornton Wilder's novel *The Bridge of San Luis Rey*.

At intervals of a day's march along the roads were *tambos*, or way stations, which offered accommodations for travelers and also stocked food, supplies and weapons for soldiers on the march. Some *tambos* were equipped with fine lodgings which were kept ready for the Inca to use during tours of inspection. There were also huts at more frequent intervals which were used by the *chasquis*, or runners, who were stationed throughout the empire as a fleet-footed messenger service. Intelligence from all parts of the realm was brought to the Inca by runners with greater reliability than the telegraph can manage in some parts of the same areas today. The runners memorized their messages and passed them on orally. Runners also brought fruit and game from the tropics and fish from the Pacific for the Inca's table.

The diversity of religions was one of the lesser problems. The Incas' religion was not exclusive. Gods worshiped by subject peoples were simply incorporated into the Inca pantheon—although Viracocha and the sun god, Inti, remained superior.

POPULATION and tribute records were kept meticulously, probably more carefully than census and tax figures are kept in the Andean countries today. The Incas had a passion for keeping track of things, whether people, food, wool or stones for their slings, and they did it with a curious device called the *quipu*, a system of knotted strings used for recording numerical information. To a horizontal cord were attached vertical strings. On the vertical strings were complexes of knots, arranged to represent numbers in a decimal system. The *quipu* was made more versatile by use of different colors, textures and thicknesses of strings. It may even have been possible to use the *quipu* for recording history, or at least that part of history which is concerned with dates, sequences of events and numbers of items.

The 16th Century Spaniards heard from Inca sages that in one of their early periods the Andean peoples had had a system of writing, but that it had been suppressed through conquest and when revived had been banned as a suspected source of pestilence, superstition and vice. The Peruvian banker-archeologist Rafael Larco Hoyle, whose private museum of pre-Columbian artifacts is one of the world's greatest, believes that some of the Andean people used dots and lines, which they incised on dry beans, in what may have been an approach to a written language.

THIS apparent lack of a developed system of writing is all the more surprising in view of the richness of the Quechua language. It is one with many nuances; it is adaptable to the expression of abstract ideas and is beautiful when used in poetry or song. Speaking Quechua today is a matter of pride among Indians in the Andean countries and also among a great many non-Indians, including scholars, merchants and missionaries. The traveler in the highlands should be prepared for the Quechua-speaking mestizo who will, with or without invitation, recite Quechua poetry, translate it into Spanish and demand, rhetorically, to know which is the more beautiful tongue. A Bolivian diplomat, who has spent most of his life abroad, was cared for as a child by a Quechua-speaking nurse, and he has never forgotten the language. "My Spanish is full of Gallicisms and Anglicisms," he says wryly, "but, thank God, my Quechua has remained pure."

It is a difficult language. A man who had learned Quechua as a child was engaged to teach a course in English at the university in Potosí, Bolivia. The university was at the time being swept by a tide of anti-Yankeeism, and some of the students rebelled at learning "the language of the imperialists." "Very well," the teacher said, "I shall teach you Quechua instead," and began to do so. After one day of intricate Quechua grammar and pronunciation the students went to the rector and begged to be allowed to study English.

Although it has become so through use, "Quechua" was not the correct name of the language. The Quechua were one of the tribes in the Cuzco area that the Incas subjugated, and the use of their name for the language, which was really the language of the Inca people, was probably due to an error on the part of one of the chroniclers. The Incas called their language not Quechua but Runa Simi, or the tongue of mankind—which is precisely what they made it in their empire. It was Inca policy to cause as little disruption as possible in the lives of a subjugated people, who were therefore allowed to speak their own tongue. But colonists speaking the language of the Incas were brought in from other parts of the empire to live among them, and groups of people from newly conquered tribes would be sent to other parts of the empire where help was needed. At the same time, children of the chief and head men of vanquished tribes were taken to Cuzco for education, not only in Quechua but in other ways of the Incas. This interchange rapidly spread not only the language but other Inca institutions as well. Of all the languages of the peoples conquered by the Incas, only that of the Aymara, natives of southern Peru and western Bolivia, survived and is spoken today.

INCA laws were simple. The basic commandments were against murder, stealing, lying, laziness and dissolute living. All were punishable by death. Brother-sister marriages were standard for the ruling Incas but forbidden others. Concubinage was common for rulers and nobility (some Incas were said to have had as many as 700 wives), but the first wife held a privileged position and could not be divorced. Gold, believed to be tears wept by the sun, belonged to the state and was used for the adornment of temples. There was no money, nor any need for it. Goods were traded by barter at three market days each month. After the trading was over, there would be music played on flutes, panpipes and drums, dancing and much drinking of *chicha,* a fermented maize drink. Llamas and guinea pigs were sacrificed to propitiate the gods and for soothsaying. Human sacrifice was practiced on extraordinary occasions, but never in the wholesale lots that it was, for instance, among the Aztecs.

There was a simple sort of folk wisdom, expressed in sayings attributed to various Inca rulers, which survived the tumult of Spanish rule, such as: "Ambition does not enrich, but impoverishes the mind, for it deprives it of the advice of honest people";

"Envy is a worm that gnaws and consumes the entrails of ambitious men"; and "The peace of a nation comes from the obedience of all its subjects."

Except for the notable achievements in organization and engineering the Incas did not invent or create much of lasting import. They were skilled in ceramics and textiles and in working with gold and silver, copper and bronze. But in the main their contribution as artisans was the refinement and technological improvement of methods and styles that had been originated and developed by earlier Andean peoples.

THERE was, however, an exception. In architecture the Incas used methods and styles that became peculiarly their own. Enough examples have survived to excite wonder today—the stately city of Machu Picchu on the brow of a remote Andean peak, the fortress of Sacsahuaman on the outskirts of Cuzco, and the foundations and walls of numerous buildings in the heart of Cuzco. The style is massive. Huge pieces of granite, porphyry and other Andean stone were hewn with stone tools into building blocks with complex and intricate combinations of angles. The huge blocks (one of them, at Sacsahuaman, measures 38 by 18 by 6 feet) were cut out of the mountains, maneuvered to the building site and elevated into position with neither draft animals nor any mechanical device more complicated than a lever. The blocks were fitted together without mortar so snugly that neither earthquakes nor centuries of neglect have shifted them. Many of the stone walls were once dressed with gold and silver plate (which the Spaniards, of course, removed), but there was little other decoration. Inca buildings make up in grandeur and dignity what they may lack in elaborate design. It is as though it satisfied the builders to cut up the stone of the unruly mountains into disciplined shapes and rearrange them in more pleasing and useful forms, suitable symbols of a great and powerful empire. The greatest of the Incas' architectural achievements were in Cuzco, the capital. Pedro de Cieza de León, a thoughtful and observant 16th Century Spanish soldier who became one of the best chroniclers of Peru, thought Cuzco had an "air of nobility" unmatched in the New World, and that "those who founded it must have been people of great worth."

The Incas and Their Ancestors

A series of extraordinary cultures flourished in the Andean world before the coming of the Spaniards. Although much of the art and architecture of these "heathen" civilizations was destroyed by the Christian colonizers, much also remains. Inca walls still stand, often forming parts of later buildings, and portions of the Inca road network can still be used. Recently archeologists have been uncovering more and more ruins and artifacts which indicate that the region's pre-Inca peoples had remarkable artistic and engineering skills. In the meantime, missionaries and anthropologists have become familiar with the present-day Indian tribes of the interior—whose way of life remains far more primitive than that of the Incas' predecessors, who lived two millennia ago.

CELEBRATED WALL in Cuzco, Peru, containing a carefully beveled "twelve-angled stone" *(above, right),* looks down on a burden-bearing Indian. The wall was part of an Inca palace.

ANCIENT THOROUGHFARE, Cuzco's Calle San Andres is lined by Inca walls, one now topped with Spanish balconies. Cuzco was the Inca capital, and much Inca masonry has survived.

COMPLEX STRUCTURES form part of the Inca city of Machu Picchu *(opposite).* Inca masons used no cement, but fitted stones so carefully that many walls remain intact after 500 years.

*STARK RIDGES high
in the Peruvian Andes
surround the magnificent
Inca fortress-city
of Machu Picchu*

FABULOUS "LOST" CITY used by the
last Inca ruler as an impregnable refuge
from Pizarro and his conquistadors clings
to a ridge 2,000 feet above the Urubamba
Valley 50 miles from Cuzco, Peru. Abandoned after the Spanish conquest and unknown for centuries, Machu Picchu was
discovered by the U.S. archeologist Hiram
Bingham in 1911. This picture of the
Inca stronghold was made from an airplane
whose pilot braved the treacherous mountain air currents to make possible a unique-
ly dramatic photograph by Cornell Capa.

35

Fantastic face grins from a still brightly colored piece of textile woven by Indians in Peru sometime between 300 B.C. and 200 A.D.

Pottery by Moche people dates from before 800 A.D.

PRE-INCA CULTURES produced some
remarkable pottery and textiles,
the equal of any made in ancient Egypt

Animal jar shows the Nazca pottery style (100-700 A.D.).

Moche portrait jar antedates Incas by some 400 years.

Fanciful jug is a relic of the Wari culture (about 1000 A.D.).

Club-wielding man (left) is in the early Salinar style.

37

THE IMPRESSIVE RELICS of
the pre-Inca past are being discovered and studied by archeologists

IMMENSE FIGURE of a monkey 90 yards long lies on a rock-strewn Peruvian plain. The figure was made by the Nazca people, who removed stones, leaving a design in the gravel below.

ENORMOUS CARVED STONE tops the 15-foot-high "Gateway of the Sun" at the famous ruins of Tiahuanaco in Bolivia. The central figure is apparently Viracocha, the god of creation.

MAZELIKE WALLS at Tiahuanaco *(left),* built before 1000 A.D., are crossed by a cyclist. The walls originally supported a stone platform. The site is famed for its statues *(foreground).*

BUSY ARCHEOLOGIST, Frederic Engel, a French businessman and amateur digger, examines the bones of a girl who was buried in Peru's arid Paracas peninsula some 8,500 years ago.

ABORIGINES in the jungles of eastern Peru live a tribal life far more primitive than that of many pre-Inca peoples

STRAW-HATTED INDIAN of the Amahuaca tribe, his face painted with dye, fingers one of the arrows he uses to kill small game. His village, Varadero, has 20 Indian households.

YOUTHFUL HUNTER, a 12-year-old Amahuaca boy named Pansitimba *(below)* fastens a feather to an arrow shaft. He lives in Varadero, the largest village of his tribe in Peru.

AGILE CLIMBER, an Amahuaca tribesman named Maponhni works his way up a tree trunk with the aid of a cloth wrapped around his feet to recover the body of a bird he has shot. The Amahuaca tribesmen must hunt constantly to assure a supply of food.

FACIAL DECORATION of red dye is stippled onto the cheek of a young Amahuaca hunter by his sister. The Amahuaca wear lip buttons made of metal from a plane that crashed nearby.

ARROW MAKER, an Amahuaca *(below)* spins a shaft to test its balance. The Stone Age way of life of these Indians will change as Peru seeks to develop its eastern lowland provinces.

A massive adobe gate marks the entrance to the Monte Sierpe hacienda, established near Pisco, Peru, in colonial times. Two foremen cros

a field irrigated by streams flowing down from the Andes beyond.

3

The Violent Disruption

IN the northern Peruvian town of Cajamarca on August 29, 1533, the "black legend" of Spain won a firm place in the history of iniquity. A group of hardheaded Spanish ruffians—one historian called them "the scum of Spanish chivalry"—listened while their fanatical spiritual adviser, Fray Vicente de Valverde, prayed for the soul of an Indian. The Indian, Atahuallpa, was the ruler of a vast realm to which the Spaniards proposed to bring Christianity and enlightenment. He had invited the Spaniards to occupy Cajamarca. He had tried to satisfy their lust for gold and silver. In return he was accused, judged and convicted on charges that were as cloudy as the background of his accusers. He was sentenced to death by burning.

Through the intercession of Fray Vicente, who later was to be elevated to the bishopric of Cuzco, Atahuallpa was given the option of being executed by garroting instead of burning if he accepted the Christian religion. Atahuallpa agreed to become a Christian because according to his own religion anyone destroyed by earthly fire could not in the afterlife be accepted by his father, the sun. He was accordingly baptized and given the name "Juan." Then a Spanish soldier slipped a noose around his neck, placed a stick in the noose and twisted it until the stoic Indian fell dead.

Atahuallpa's Indian followers intoned a lament: *"Chaupi punchapi tutayaca"* (Night has fallen at noon). It was at once an elegy for their ruler, a requiem for the well-ordered Inca Empire, and a prologue to one of the bitterest and bloodiest eras in the annals of conquest and exploration. Within 15 years the principal Spanish leaders in the conquest of Peru would be dead, victims of rivalry, greed and civil wars. The lucky ones would die on battlefields, fighting their fellow Spaniards more often than Indians. The others would be assassinated, drawn and quartered, or beheaded, their heads stuck on pikestaffs and exhibited in the principal plazas of the area the Spaniards called New Castile. Most of them would have found the wealth they so desperately sought—and lost it.

T HAT these fortune seekers and empire builders were indifferent to human life—the lives of the Indians or even those of their fellow Spaniards—was not particularly remarkable in that age of conquest. Nevertheless, some of the conquistadors themselves felt shame and repugnance, and the Spanish Crown tried at various times to curb the rapacity of the overseas adventurers, as did the Church. Many of the priests who came out to the New World with the expeditionary forces became noted as both teachers and defenders of the Indians, but their efforts in behalf of the natives stirred furious resentment among the conquistadors. Most of them felt that since priests invariably accompanied them and gave them spiritual comfort during their campaigns against the Indians, they therefore had religious sanction for any extremes to which they might go in subduing the heathen and in the course of it enriching themselves with plunder.

Almost all of the conquistadors were poor men, and they came from a poor country. Spain, always short on material resources, had been particularly impoverished by centuries of wars against the Moors. These wars had molded the Spanish character and had made it long on courage and a curious sense of

honor and short on a feeling for humanity. Military achievement was the road to advancement, even for the most humble. Respectability came to be measured in gold, land and slaves. The Spanish soldier of fortune never ceased dreaming of them, and considered them his just rewards for enduring the privations and dangers of colonial conquest.

These 16th Century Spaniards, ill-educated for the most part, were convinced that the little-known world of their day hid countless wonders: cities of gold and enchantment, fountains of youth, tribes of beautiful women warriors. And there were countless races of rich but benighted people waiting for Christianity and the Spanish yoke. The exotic land and the treasures in gold, silver and gems that Hernán Cortés and his swashbuckling companions had found—and seized—in Mexico gave substance to these dreams.

The story of the Spanish invasion of the Andean region begins in 1511, when Vasco Núñez de Balboa, a typical Spanish soldier of fortune who was then in Central America, became the first white man to hear of Peru. A native chief, watching Balboa count gold that had been taken from the Indians, expressed surprise at his interest in such stuff. There was, he said, a land far to the south where people had gold in abundance and held it in no more esteem than the Spaniards did iron. Later, on the shores of the Pacific Ocean, which he discovered and claimed for Spain, Balboa heard of Peru once more. His informant also drew a picture of a strange animal, a native of the country to the south. It looked like a sheep with the head and neck of a camel. It was called a llama.

H ERE were the ingredients—a strange, far land full of gold, heathens and odd beasts—that could galvanize the legend-susceptible Spaniard and put him on the path of exploration. But little was done about it for more than a decade, and Balboa was to play no part in the conquest of Peru. For the most part the Spaniards in Panama were exploring to the north and west, trying to find a waterway between the Atlantic and the Pacific. It was not until after Cortés overcame the opulent Aztec Empire in Mexico that the Spaniards began seriously to consider the mysterious lands to the south.

In 1524 two Spanish soldiers of fortune, Francisco Pizarro and Diego de Almagro, and a schoolteacher-priest, Hernando de Luque, formed a compact for an expedition to Peru. Luque was to raise funds for the expedition (he was only a front for the real investor, a lawyer named Gaspar de Espinosa). Almagro was to be in charge of supplies and equipment. And Pizarro was to lead the expedition—or expeditions, for there were to be three. The first, begun late that year, was short and unproductive.

THE second voyage, after many difficulties, reached the ninth degree south of the equator, below the present-day location of Trujillo, Peru. In the course of the expedition Pizarro and some of his men spent a miserable season on the desolate island of Gallo, while the ships returned to Panama for supplies and reinforcements. The stay on Gallo produced a near-mutiny. At a critical moment Pizarro drew a line in the sand with his sword and, according to legend, faced south and told his men: "On that side are toil, hunger, nakedness, the drenching storm, desertion, and death; on this side, ease and pleasure. There lies Peru with its riches; here, Panamá and its poverty. Choose, each man, what best becomes a brave Castilian. For my part, I go to the south." And he stepped across the line—to be followed by 13 others who were to become known in Spanish history books as "The Thirteen of Fame." It was a characteristic action in an age much given to dramatic and chivalric gestures.

At Tumbes, on the Peruvian coast, Pizarro and his men found a well-built city, with gold-decorated temples and a finely garbed aristocracy who drank and ate from golden utensils. The Spaniards were told that in the capital of the country, a beautiful city on a faraway mountain plain, there was much more gold and silver. After a peaceful stay in Tumbes and some further exploration the Spaniards, convinced that they had found a rich and promising kingdom, returned to Panama with a modest fortune in gold and silver, some natives to be trained as interpreters, some llamas—which the Spaniards called "sheep of Peru"—and a sampling of the fine textiles woven in this strange country.

The returning adventurers were greeted warmly by their friends in Panama, many of whom had given them up for lost. But their appeals to the Governor of the colony, Pedro de los Ríos, for support and aid in mounting an expedition of conquest were coldly received. The Governor's reason probably was that he feared development of a new colony that might eclipse his own. He deplored the loss of men on the Pizarro expeditions, ridiculed the gold, silver and "sheep" that Pizarro had brought back, and refused to give any help.

Having failed to get any support from the Panamanian Governor, Pizarro set out for Spain. A one-time swineherd, Pizarro was illiterate and remained so all his life, but he was an impressive man and could speak convincingly on subjects he knew. He evidently convinced the Spanish Queen, who, acting for King Charles V, signed a "capitulation" that gave Pizarro the rank of Governor and Captain-General of Peru. He was also assigned a handsome salary to be taken from whatever revenue the future colony would produce. He was admitted to the knightly Order of Santiago and was authorized to launch an expedition of conquest. Whatever adventurers he could recruit for the project were to bear the costs—together with Pizarro's creditors. Aside from a few military supplies the Spanish Crown was venturing nothing.

IN search of recruits, Pizarro visited his birthplace, the town of Trujillo in Spain's Estremadura province. Among those whom he persuaded to come along were three of his brothers: Hernando, Juan and Gonzalo Pizarro. He also enlisted Francisco Martín de Alcántara, a half brother on his mother's side. Of the three Pizarros only one, Hernando, was the acknowledged son of his father; the others were illegitimate, as was Francisco himself.

Pizarro returned to Panama and in January 1531 sailed on his final expedition. He had three small vessels, 180 men and 27 horses. His old associate, Diego de Almagro, remained behind in Panama to drum up reinforcements. On the first two expeditions Pizarro had been circumspect, where possible, in his treatment of the natives. Now he plundered as he went, sending back supplies of gold and jewels to Panama to speed the recruiting of additional men and to satisfy his creditors. He and his men were welcomed to the island of Puná in the Gulf of

Guayaquil but ended by massacring the natives for a supposed plot. They landed at Tumbes, which had excited their admiration and cupidity on the second expedition, but found it in ruins, the gold and most of the people gone and the survivors hostile. There had been local wars, Pizarro learned. And more important, he was told that the Inca Empire itself was split by dissension, since it was ruled by two brothers, each of whom had his own realm. Pizarro knew from Cortés' experience in Mexico that the Spaniards' greatest ally was native disunity.

Pizarro marched south to the banks of the Piura River and established a settlement which was to be his base of operations. He built a fortress, a church and a storehouse and parceled out land and Indians to his followers. Gold and silver booty was melted down and sent back to Panama. A base party was stationed at San Miguel, as the new town was called, and in September 1532 the Spaniards marched inland toward the heart of the Inca Empire.

THE empire, the largest and most cohesive one ever organized in aboriginal America, had begun to come apart. The trend toward disunity had begun under Huayna Capac, 11th in the line of Inca rulers. He was the grandson and son respectively of Pachacuti and Topa Yupanqui, who had done more than any other Incas to expand the empire and to govern it with efficiency and justice.

Huayna was an unorthodox ruler. He had questioned the omnipotence of the sun and thereby outraged his priests. Where his ancestors had treated conquered Indian tribes with respect, even gentleness, he was harsh. Some of his prisoners he marked by extracting their front teeth as a symbol of defeat. Others were impaled and cut to pieces. He also violated tradition by marrying the daughter of the last ruler of Quito, a kingdom the Incas had conquered, and installing her in a place of favor in his palace in Quito. Polygamy was common, and the Inca rulers fathered many sons by many wives, but only the first wife held a queenly position. Huayna not only favored Paccha, the Quito Princess, over his first wife, but also preferred Atahuallpa, the son of this union, to Huáscar, the son who normally would succeed him. It was Atahuallpa whom the Spaniards later garroted in Cajamarca.

When Huayna felt that his end was near in 1525, he performed his most unorthodox act of all. He divided the realm between the two sons. Atahuallpa was to govern the northern empire, with its capital at Quito, while Huáscar was to rule what was left of the traditional Inca Empire, with its capital at Cuzco. In an empire that had been tightly unified it was an untenable arrangement, and war was not long in breaking out between the two brothers. Atahuallpa camped near Cajamarca while the main body of his troops marched on to Cuzco and defeated those of Huáscar. Atahuallpa was still at Cajamarca when Pizarro and his army of less than 200 men arrived after a perilous march up into the mountains from their base on the coast.

Whether Pizarro and his small force could have overcome an undivided Inca Empire is open to question. The Spaniards had firearms, horses and steel armor, which gave them an advantage of perhaps 100 to 1, perhaps even 1,000 to 1. But they were confronting a nation that could have put hundreds of thousands of warriors in the field, men who could be deadly accurate with stones hurled from six-foot slings, with lariats and bolas, with spears and war clubs tipped with stone or bronze. They were warriors trained from childhood to be ready to die for their ruler, the Inca. But now a flaw had appeared in the imperial structure. The awesome authority of the Inca had been divided. There was confusion and uneasiness in the masses of the people and, apparently, in the mind of Atahuallpa himself, victorious though he had been in his war with Huáscar. His hospitable treatment of the strange white men may well have been due to his fear that they might make league against him with his half brother. While he was a captive of the Spaniards, Atahuallpa sent word secretly to his people ordering the execution of the captive Huáscar.

IT was Atahuallpa's own suggestion that he free himself through ransom. He had noted the Spaniards' mania for gold and silver—metals which the Incas valued only for their decorative qualities and religious connotations. He was imprisoned in a cell which (according to the various chroniclers) was either 22 or 25 or 35 feet long by either 15 or 17 feet wide. He would, he said, order his people to fill the

room with gold from all parts of the realm in exchange for his freedom, and he would have two more rooms filled with silver. The Spaniards were delighted, and Atahuallpa quickly sent messengers out to all corners of the empire. Soon loads of precious metal began to arrive on the backs of llamas and human carriers—statues, vessels, personal ornaments and great sheets of bulk metal from temple walls.

Estimates of the value of the ransom have ranged as high as $20 million. But in 1938 the American archeologist Samuel K. Lothrop, after a careful study of all the records and commentaries and a correlation of Spanish weights and measures to those of the present day, computed a value of $8,344,307 for it. Lothrop also figured Pizarro's subsequent booty in Cuzco at $8,545,798.57, a grand total of nearly $17 million (compared with only a little more than one million dollars in treasure seized by Cortés in Mexico). Nor was this to be the end of the loot. Hoards of precious metal were later found in temples, in graves and at building sites. However, the Spaniards and their descendants were taunted by surviving Indians with hints that the gold and silver they had found were as one grain to a whole basketful. For, they said, when word of Atahuallpa's fate got abroad in the empire many caravans laden with treasure were still en route to Cajamarca. The caravans were stopped and the gold and silver cached in lakes and caves and lonely places where, with luck, the white man would never find them. It was a revenge of sorts, because nothing could make the Spaniards so miserable as the knowledge of inaccessible treasure.

Atahuallpa was, of course, killed anyway, regardless of Spanish promises and all the gold and silver that had been delivered. In spite of the mock legal process by which he was condemned and executed it appears that the real reason for his execution was that the Spaniards could not think of anything else to do with him. This treacherous deed established in the Indian mind a distrust of the white man that, in the centuries that followed, grew until it became instinct; and the Indians' *desconfianza*, an inborn sense of distrust, is one of the divisive elements in the Andean world today.

The quick wealth that had fallen so easily into their hands did the Spaniards little good. It stimulated greed and jealousy and set one conquistador against another. It resulted in the ruin of most of them and in time helped to destroy Spain as a power in the New World.

Of all the rivalries among the Spaniards the one of longest standing, and in the end the most violent, was that between Francisco Pizarro and Diego de Almagro, the original partners in the venture. Although Almagro had been an equal partner with Pizarro in the explorations to the south, he had been consistently given the less glamorous jobs—finding ships and matériel and men, sailing back and forth with reinforcements, arms and supplies. When Pizarro had returned to Spain after the second expedition, he had secured for himself various honors and the promise of titles, to be effective when the proposed colony of New Castile came into existence. For his partner, Almagro, he got nothing but the conditional appointment as commander of the non-existent fortress-to-be at Tumbes. But by the time Pizarro reached Tumbes the once-impressive Indian town had been destroyed by the natives. The first Spanish fortress was built elsewhere, and there was no title for Almagro. He arrived at Cajamarca with needed reinforcements before the execution of Atahuallpa but apparently did not get his proper share of the Inca's ransom.

Despite these disappointments Almagro carried on as a good soldier. He took the field against the fiercest surviving Inca chieftain, Quizquiz, and defeated him. He marched to Ecuador, where a veteran of the Mexican campaign, Pedro de Alvarado, was trying to lay claim to a part of the rich new South American empire, and persuaded him to withdraw. However, while he continued to obey orders and maintained an appearance of friendship with Pizarro, Almagro no longer trusted his old partner; and when Hernando Pizarro, Francisco's brother, returned to Spain in 1533 with part of the expedition's loot, Almagro took the precaution of sending a confidential agent to watch the way he behaved at the court. For once a Pizarro behaved honorably and pressed Almagro's claims as well as his own. The King, mollified by the treasure laid before him, granted Almagro authority to conquer and govern territory, to be called New Toledo, for a distance of 200 leagues to the south of Francisco Pizarro's New Castle. At the same time the King extended Pizarro's colony by 70 leagues, to a total of 270.

The point of departure for such measurements was the island of Puná, which lies offshore near the present boundary between Ecuador and Peru. Spanish measurements were anything but precise. The southern dividing line between the territories of Pizarro and Almagro lay somewhere close to the old Inca capital of Cuzco, so close that authority over the city became a cause of contention—and eventually of civil war. The confusion that beset the conquerors has plagued the Andean countries ever since in their disputes over boundaries.

An immediate clash over Cuzco was averted by Almagro's expedition into the southern part of New

---

THE EMBATTLED ARAUCANIANS

Chile's Araucanian Indians fought the encroaching white man from the moment the Europeans appeared in Chile in the 16th Century until the latter years of the 19th. Warlike and brave, the Araucanians were a very primitive people, especially compared with the Incas. They lived in small, isolated communities except in times of war and built no great cities. Primarily hunters, they spent little time tilling the soil. Their dwellings were rude, one-room huts made of poles, animal hides and straw. The Araucanians' language was highly developed, however, and they prided themselves on their oratorical ability. They loved games, especially *chueca*, a rugged sport akin to field hockey. Today's Araucanians still tend to live apart on their traditional lands, but they are much better farmers than their ancestors were and raise large herds of cattle.

Toledo, today's Chile. It was an arduous operation and a disappointing one. No gold was found, and the natives were more hostile than the Incas. Almagro returned to Peru to press his claim for Cuzco. Gonzalo and Hernando Pizarro had been left in charge there by Francisco while the latter went off to build his capital on the present site of Lima.

Almagro seized Cuzco and imprisoned Gonzalo and Hernando Pizarro, bringing on a civil war. In the final battle of this war, at Las Salinas, Almagro was decisively defeated. Groups of Indians, with impartial pleasure, gathered on the nearby mountainsides to watch Spaniards killing Spaniards. Almagro, old and ill with syphilis, was finally captured, garroted and beheaded. The Pizarro brothers, who had done the same for Atahuallpa, piously donned mourning apparel for the funeral services.

But this was not to be the end of the Almagro-Pizarro feud. Almagro's son by a Panamanian Indian woman, a youth who had accompanied his father on his campaigns and was known as Almagro the Boy, carried on the dispute. He became the center of a conspiracy among his father's followers —known as "The Men of Chile"—that ended in a bold assault on Francisco Pizarro's palace in Lima and the assassination of the principal leader of the conquest of Peru. The plotters then proclaimed young Almagro Governor, but he was subsequently forced to relinquish the post when a new Governor was sent out from Spain. Later he was defeated in the Battle of Chupas and was, as seemed to be the custom, beheaded in the square at Cuzco.

The Pizarros fared as badly as had the Almagros. Even before the assassination of Francisco, Juan Pizarro had been fatally wounded in a battle with rebellious Indians outside of Cuzco. Francisco Martín de Alcántara, Francisco Pizarro's half brother, fell in the same attack in which Francisco was killed.

Hernando, the best-educated and most courtly of the Pizarros, managed to return to Spain but spent the next 20 years of his life in prison for the collective misdeeds of his brothers.

The remaining brother, Gonzalo, was perhaps the most violent and venturesome of the lot. He was a fearless fighter and a courageous explorer. As Governor of Quito he set off on a disastrous expedition into eastern Ecuador. When Gonzalo struggled back to Quito he found that his brother Francisco had been assassinated, and he was forced to accept the authority of a Viceroy sent out from Spain. Like many of the other conquistadors, he resisted Spain's so-called "New Laws," which were intended to ameliorate the lot of Peru's Indians. He headed a rebellious movement that led to the death of the Viceroy and then served as Governor of what was briefly an independent Peru. Forces loyal to the Crown took the field against him in another civil war. Finally he was deserted by his own men on the battlefield and, like so many others, was beheaded.

THE record of the Spaniards in South America was not all black. There were noble and just men among them. Hernando de Soto, who was later to discover the Mississippi River, came to Peru in one of the first groups of reinforcements to reach Pizarro. He proved to be one of the bravest soldiers in the conquest and also one of the most decent, particularly in his dealings with the Indians. He befriended Atahuallpa and made every effort to save him from execution at Cajamarca.

Another of the exemplary Spaniards was Pedro de la Gasca, a gentle-mannered ecclesiastic who was sent out from Spain with plenipotentiary powers to restore order after the anarchy created by the Pizarros and their followers. He proved himself to be a valiant soldier, a tough-minded administrator, and one of the few Spaniards who did not try to enrich themselves at the expense of their comrades or the Indians.

But in sum, the heritage of the conquistadors was one of disunity, dissension and destruction—from some of which the Andean world still has not recovered. "Whatever can be burned is burned," wrote one of the chroniclers, explaining the Spaniards' efforts to stamp out idolatry, "the rest is broken." It extended to more than idolatry—which was of a mild sort as idolatries go. The carefully regulated Inca system of social justice was destroyed. The magnificent Inca roads and irrigation systems fell into disrepair. The Inca methods of getting the greatest possible agricultural production from a country of limited resources were disrupted and forgotten. The Indians were accustomed to stern rule under the Inca chiefs, but they knew that their obligations to the Inca and Inca-administered justice were both certain and unvarying. Under the Spaniards, there was no limit to their obligations, and justice was reserved for the white man.

WILLIAM HICKLING PRESCOTT, the great American historian who more than a century ago wrote what has remained the definitive account of the conquest of Peru, lamented: ". . . he [Pizarro] found a country well advanced in the arts of civilization; institutions under which the people lived in tranquillity and personal safety; the mountains and the uplands whitened with flocks; the valleys teeming with the fruits of a scientific husbandry; the granaries and warehouses filled to overflowing; the whole land rejoicing in its abundance; and the character of the nation, softened under the influence of the mildest and most innocent form of superstition, well prepared for the reception of a higher and Christian civilization. But, far from introducing this, Pizarro delivered up the conquered races to his brutal soldiery; the sacred cloisters were abandoned to their lust; the towns and villages were given up to pillage; the wretched natives were parceled out like slaves, to toil for their conquerors in the mines; the flocks were scattered and wantonly destroyed; the granaries were dissipated; the beautiful contrivances for the more perfect culture of the soil were suffered to fall into decay; the paradise was converted into a desert. Instead of profiting by the ancient forms of civilization, Pizarro preferred to efface every vestige of them from the land, and on their ruin to erect the institutions of his own country. Yet these institutions did little for the poor Indian, held in iron bondage. It was little to him that the shores of the Pacific were studded with rising communities and cities, the marts of a flourishing commerce. He had no share in the goodly heritage. He was an alien in the land of his fathers."

A Rich Treasure
of New World Art

The Spaniards who took so much wealth from the New World gave in return a priceless heritage of art and architecture which still illuminates the Andean countries. European styles of building and painting, especially the baroque and rococo, were transported to the colonies, and important schools of painting flourished in Quito and Cuzco. The elaborate work of these schools can be seen today in the churches and museums of all the Andean countries. Especially ardent guardians of this tradition are the aristocratic families that trace their lineage back to the early settlers. Many of their splendid houses are veritable show places of the New World's lustrous cultural heritage.

CHOIR STALLS in the Church of San Francisco in Quito, Ecuador, are decorated with fine wood carvings. The church, begun about 1537, was the first baroque cathedral in the New World.

STONE CARVING of an avenging angel in Inca dress, done in a Spanish rococo style known as *churrigueresco*, decorates San Lorenzo Church in Potosí, Bolivia. It was carved about 1730.

FRANCISCAN FRIAR, Brother Nicholas Pazmino of the San Francisco monastery in Quito holds a prized sculpture showing the coronation of the Virgin Mary.

RELIGIOUS PAINTINGS line a hallway in the San Francisco monastery. Some are by Miguel de Santiago, founder of the Quito school of painting in the 17th Century.

AN ARISTOCRATIC FAMILY *preserves*
four centuries of tradition in one house

CONQUISTADOR'S DESCENDANT, Luis de Aliaga of Lima sits below a portrait of an ancestor, Captain Jerónimo de Aliaga, one of Francisco Pizarro's officers during the conquest of Peru.

ELEGANT DOORWAY of the Aliaga house in Lima silhouettes Gonzalo de Aliaga, Luis' son. The house, built by Jerónimo de Aliaga in 1536, is the oldest colonial residence in South America.

HUGE LIVING ROOM of the house is filled with art and furniture imported from Spain, France, England and China in the 17th and 18th Centuries. In the center is a gilded bronze stove.

SOMBER DINING ROOM boasts an old carved cedar ceiling *(opposite)*. The Aliaga family, at the table, often dines together and remains, after the Spanish fashion, a close-knit group.

RARE COLLECTION of colonial art fills a private house near Lima

FIGURE OF CHRIST, a wood-and-silver carving of the 17th Century, is in the gallery of Lima aristocrat Pedro de Osma.

COAT OF ARMS of Osma *(below)* is a composite of the coats of arms of the four noble Spanish families in his ancestry.

GILDED RETABLE, part of a church altar, is a splendidly elaborate example of 17th and 18th Century Peruvian rococo religious art.

DEDICATED COLLECTOR, Pedro de Osma stands amid works of art that fill the 44 rooms of his house in Barranca, a Lima suburb.

Uncertain Freedom

URING one of the wild battles of the South American war for independence a hard-riding cavalryman was struck in the arm with a musket ball. The arm was shattered and had to be amputated under primitive battlefield conditions, without anesthetic. The soldier endured the operation with grim impatience. When it was finished he seized the severed arm, waved it over his head and shouted *"Viva la patria!"* But within a few days he was dead of gangrene.

The incident of the quixotic cavalryman was characteristic of the struggle that rocked South America and particularly the Andean nations from 1810 to 1824. It was a period of merciless violence and unprecedented valor, of lofty hopes and bitter reality.

The upheaval began shortly after Napoleon's invasion of Spain in 1808 had removed the Spanish King from the throne. With the King deposed and most of Spain ruled by France the Viceroys and Governors of Spain's American colonies were in a dubious position of authority. The citizens of several colonies seized the moment to set up governments of their own. These unrelated movements toward self-government were resisted by the bodies of Spanish troops stationed in the various colonies. The result was a protracted, vicious and heroic civil war. Ill-equipped patriot armies, led as often by egocentric dandies and idealistic intellectuals as by trained soldiers, performed astounding feats. Hungry and poorly clad, they marched back and forth through the icy passes of the Andes. They fought battles above the clouds, in miasmic swamps, in burning deserts. They sustained defeats that surely would have crushed lesser men; but in the decisive battles, from Chacabuco in Chile to Ayacucho in Peru, they sent the Spanish armies, superior in arms and training, reeling in defeat. Their battle cries helped shape a proud heritage.

But for the most part the postwar fortunes of the newly formed independent republics were unhappy. The tyranny of Spain was replaced by chaos and anarchy. The heroes of the battles for independence became outcasts, remembering their days of glory in lonely exile. Their hopes turned to despair and their brave words to mockery.

THERE had been a kind of peace in Spain's South American colonies for almost 300 years, maintained by Viceroys sent out to rule in the name of the King. It was a peace in which power was held by an aristocratic minority, mostly Spanish-born. The Creoles, or native-born whites, had less power, fewer privileges. The mass of the population, the Indians and mestizos, had neither power nor privilege.

But it was not uninterrupted peace. Less than 25 years after the arrival of the Spanish conquistadors, Gonzalo Pizarro, last of the Pizarro brothers in Peru, had risen in rebellion against viceregal rule, objecting to the so-called "New Laws" which would curb the absolute authority of the conquistadors. In the course of his uprising a Viceroy was killed and Gonzalo briefly governed Peru as an independent kingdom. Eventually he was brought down by forces loyal to the Crown.

From the outset of Spanish control of Peru, there had been Indian revolts. Manco, a descendant of the Inca ruler Huayna, was enthroned by the Spaniards in 1534 as a supposedly helpless quisling ruler of the remnants of the Indian empire. He became instead a fierce rebel who mustered a force of 100,000 warriors and threatened to drive the white man out of the Andean world. Two and a half centuries later a succession of Indian leaders again tried to overthrow the Spaniards. The Peruvian cities of Cuzco and Puno were threatened, and La Paz was nearly conquered by

a besieging force of 80,000 Indians bitterly resentful of Spanish oppression.

In addition to the virtual serfdom the Spaniards imposed on the Indians, there was tight control of commerce in both goods and ideas, and this aroused the resentment of non-Indian colonials. Monopolies in most goods were reserved to the Spanish Crown. For centuries commerce was permitted solely with the mother country; only in the 18th Century had the colonies been able to trade with one another. Also irksome were the restrictions against importation of books and ideas. This in time stirred opposition among Creole and mestizo intellectuals and was an important contributory factor in the independence movement that was to come.

"We are in the darkest and farthermost corner of the world," complained a mestizo Ecuadorian writer, Eugenio Espejo, "where but a few refracted rays of the vast light that illumines the privileged regions reach us; we are without books, tools, means and instructors. . . ." Similar complaints were voiced by a onetime Jesuit, Juan Bautista Vizcardo y Guzmán, who in 1792, on the 300th anniversary of the discovery of America, published his *Letter to Spanish Americans*. He objected particularly to economic oppression: "Since men first lived together in communities for mutual benefit we are the only ones in the world whom a government forces to pay the most for necessities while obliging us to sell the products of our labor at the lowest price. We are hermetically sealed off, like a city under siege. . . ."

The intellectuals read smuggled volumes of the works of Rousseau, Hobbes, Locke, Voltaire and Diderot and circulated secretly printed Spanish translations of the French Declaration of the Rights of Man. The clandestine spread of revolutionary ideas had much to do with forming the climate of rebellion.

ALTHOUGH there was much discontent, there was little solidarity. The Indian masses lived in isolated misery. The Creoles hated both the Indians and the *peninsulares,* or natives of Spain, who were sent out to the colonies as governors, administrators, judges and clerics. The mestizos, a growing class, were allied with neither the whites on one side nor the Indians on the other. Curiously enough the almost-forgotten Inca Empire of the Indians was to take on a mystical importance in the independence movement. Some of the leaders thought that once Spanish rule was overthrown the Inca Empire should be re-established.

The Indian past was also to figure in the activities of the revolutionary society to which most of the active leaders of the war against Spain belonged. The society, the Lautaro Lodge, took the name of a famed Araucanian Indian warrior who had led his people in their fight against Spanish enslavement in Chile. It was formed in London at the beginning of the 19th Century by a venturesome Venezuelan scholar, Francisco de Miranda. Virtually all of the South American freedom fighters—notably the Venezuelan Simón Bolívar, the Argentine José de San Martín and the Chilean Bernardo O'Higgins—were to become members.

The Lautaro Lodge was established, said its statutes, "for the purpose of grouping together American gentlemen who, distinguished by the liberality of ideas and the fervor of their patriotic zeal, should work together . . . for the independence and well-being of America, devoting to this most noble end all their strength, their influence, their faculties and talents, loyally sustaining one another, laboring honorably and proceeding with justice. . . ."

Generalized as this was, it was a clear statement of revolutionary aims that all the leaders of the various independence movements in the several South American countries could subscribe to. Unfortunately, the great revolutionary effort against Spain was to be marked more by brilliant, individualistic (and often uncoordinated) leadership than it was by clarity and unanimity of purpose.

Miranda, the founder of the Lautaro Lodge, was to become identified by later Spanish American historians as the "precursor" of the independence movement, just as his disciples were to be hailed as the "liberators." He was a cosmopolite, an intellectual, a soldier and a conspirator. Miranda was born in Caracas, Venezuela, in 1750, and began wandering as a young man. He served in the American Revolution and was later evicted from Venezuela for supposedly aiding smugglers. He subsequently traveled in the United States and England and became a general in the French Revolution. At one time or another he was a protégé of Catherine the Great of Russia, a

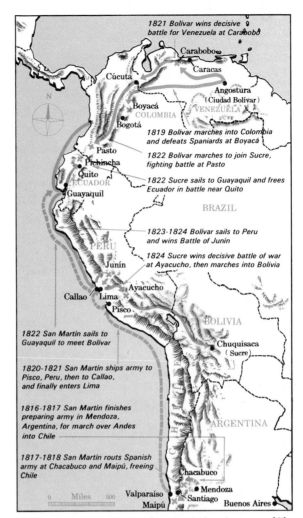

1821 Bolívar wins decisive battle for Venezuela at Carabobo

1819 Bolívar marches into Colombia and defeats Spaniards at Boyacá

1822 Bolívar marches to join Sucre, fighting battle at Pasto

1822 Sucre sails to Guayaquil and frees Ecuador in battle near Quito

1823-1824 Bolívar sails to Peru and wins Battle of Junín

1824 Sucre wins decisive battle of war at Ayacucho, then marches into Bolivia

1822 San Martín sails to Guayaquil to meet Bolívar

1820-1821 San Martín ships army to Pisco, Peru, then to Callao, and finally enters Lima

1816-1817 San Martín finishes preparing army in Mendoza, Argentina, for march over Andes into Chile

1817-1818 San Martín routs Spanish army at Chacabuco and Maipú, freeing Chile

THE GREAT CAMPAIGNS of the South American war of liberation are drawn on the map above. While the army of José de San Martín moved from the south *(broken lines)* toward Lima (the Spanish viceregal capital), Simón Bolívar and his lieutenant Sucre secured the north and then also marched on Peru *(solid lines)*. Their crucial battles are indicated by crosses.

part of the literary circle of Mme. de Staël, and an acquaintance of the British statesman William Pitt and even of Napoleon (who criticized Miranda's foppish manners but conceded that he was burning with "a sacred fire"). In England he served as a tutor to the young Irish-Chilean Bernardo O'Higgins, illegitimate son of the Viceroy of Peru, and at the same time inducted him into the Lautaro Lodge. O'Higgins, en route home to Chile, stayed for a time in Spain, and there met José de San Martín, a young Argentine aristocrat then serving in the Spanish Army. San Martín probably became a member of the revolutionary Lautaro Lodge as a result of O'Higgins' visit.

In 1806 Miranda made two attempts to launch a liberation movement in Venezuela. He received aid and equipment from U.S. and British interests which were eager to open up trade with the Spanish colonies. But the Spanish authorities learned of his first attempt in time to thwart it; the second invasion attempt was poorly organized and achieved nothing.

Despite the failure of Miranda's efforts, there was a growing sentiment for independence in Venezuela. One of the leading figures in the movement was a young man from a wealthy Creole family, Simón Bolívar. Wiry and olive-skinned, Bolívar had a presence that was at once commanding and romantic.

BOLIVAR was born in Caracas in 1783, 33 years after Miranda. He spent much of his youth on a family plantation, where he rode with the *llaneros,* or Venezuelan cowboys, and became a superb rider who, throughout his career, delighted in showing off his horsemanship. He favored fancy dress and adornment and was once arrested in Spain for wearing lace cuffs and diamond links, airs forbidden to colonials. His energy was boundless. He loved music, was a skilled and tireless dancer, and was almost as tireless in his pursuit of women—as were women in their pursuit of him. His long and open alliance with the Ecuadorian beauty Manuela Sáenz, one of the most colorful women in South American history, was the scandal of the age. His one marriage, to a girl of 16 (when he was only 18), was happy but brief; his wife died within a year of their marriage.

In addition to being a figure of considerable color and romance Bolívar was a serious student, a philosopher, a man with the emotions of a poet and the indomitable soul of a patriot. He was a prolific writer of letters, declarations and manifestoes, all both eloquent and analytic and many of them prophetic. As a child he was tutored by Simón Rodríguez, a Venezuelan radical who opened Bolívar's eyes to the social injustice of the Spanish colonial regime and introduced him to the works of many important European writers, including Rousseau, whose *Emile* was to be an important influence in Bolívar's development. Bolívar took an oath in the presence of Rodríguez: "I never shall allow my hands to be idle nor my soul to rest until I have broken the shackles that chain us to Spain." Another of Bolívar's teachers was Andrés Bello, who later, in Chile, was to become one of the leading intellectuals of 19th Century South America—a poet, educator and jurist.

Miranda, too, was to help in the shaping of Bolívar's character as a patriot and revolutionary. In 1810 a group of revolutionaries in Caracas who had established an independent junta, or governing council, sent Bolívar and his teacher Bello to London to try to win British recognition and support. In London the two visitors met Miranda, and Bolívar was strongly influenced by the older man's libertarian philosophy. At Bolívar's insistence Miranda returned to Venezuela, took charge of the revolutionary army and helped inspire the Act of Venezuelan Independence, one of the first such formal documents to be drawn up in the Spanish colonies in South America.

But Miranda's efforts were doomed. An earthquake destroyed most of Caracas and much of the Venezuelans' revolutionary ardor. Desertions reduced Miranda's army. His principal disciple, Bolívar, let a key fortress fall into royalist hands while he amused himself with music and girls. Miranda was forced to surrender and might have escaped but was turned over to the royalists by Bolívar. Bolívar, perhaps in an unconscious defense of his own shortcomings as a soldier, had decided that Miranda was a traitor to the revolutionary cause. In return for having betrayed his friend and co-plotter, Bolívar, instead of being imprisoned, was allowed to go into exile. Miranda was taken to Spain, where he died in a Cádiz dungeon.

DESPITE this inauspicious beginning, Bolívar was destined to become one of the two dominant figures in the war that was to liberate South America from Spanish rule—the other being the great Argentine, San Martín. Bolívar's formal training as a soldier was meager, and his disposition was, perhaps, too mercurial for a successful military man. He wanted power, risked everything to get it and then often neglected to exercise it. He was subject to moods of despair and deplored his fellow citizens' lack of "the political virtues that characterize true republicans." His complaints could be bitter: "We were given philosophers for leaders, philanthropy for legislation, dialectics for tactics, and sophists for soldiers." But moody and unorthodox though he may have been, he was a military genius, achieving through courage, imagination and dash victories that a more conventional soldier might have considered impossible.

After a period of brooding exile in Curaçao, Bolívar made his way back to the mainland. The town of Cartagena, on the coast of what is now Colombia, was a stronghold of the independence movement. Bolívar was given a commission as a colonel in Cartagena's makeshift forces, but proceeded to disobey orders by raising a force of his own, largely mulattoes, and setting out on an independent campaign against the Spaniards. He and his men moved up the Magdalena River, overwhelming Spanish garrisons and seizing weapons and supplies. He then turned east toward Venezuela, traversing first the torrid jungles and then the high, cold passes of the Andes. In a three-month period Bolívar and his motley troops covered 800 difficult miles, fought six battles, destroyed five Spanish military units, and captured some valuable artillery and ammunition. In August of 1813 he and his army marched grandly into Caracas, whose citizens, in gratitude, voted Bolívar the title of "Liberator."

But freedom was not so quickly won. During 1813 and 1814 Bolívar fought a score of battles in Venezuela, suffered some severe defeats and again went into exile, first in Jamaica and then in Haiti, where he promised the President of the Negro republic that he would abolish slavery in the countries that he freed.

Back in Venezuela at the end of 1816, he fought against the royalists for two years without success; then his luck began to turn. His army was strengthened by the addition of a hard-riding cavalry made up of *llaneros*, who had until then fought for the Spaniards. He also recruited many English and Irish veterans of the Napoleonic Wars who had come to South America looking for work after Napoleon's final defeat at the Battle of Waterloo. In 1819 Bolívar was

BOLIVAR'S PERSUASIVE RHETORIC

The "Liberator" Simón Bolívar had the power to put in highly colored language his sense of his own importance and the importance of his mission of liberating South America from Spanish rule. Below are two eloquent passages from his letters.

As the straight and courageous man must be indifferent to the onslaughts of ill-fortune, I am armed with constancy, and look with disdain on the shots of fate. On my heart no one has sway but my own conscience. . . .

It is in vain that arms destroy tyrants if they do not establish a political order capable of repairing the devastations of the revolution . . . we need our civil leaders, who, escaped on planks from the shipwreck of the revolution, may guide us back through the sands into a harbor of salvation.

named both President and Commander in Chief of Venezuela. Shortly thereafter he made another heroic crossing of the Andes, this time during the rainy season, and at the Colombian town of Boyacá he overwhelmed the royalists in one of the truly decisive battles of the war for independence. The grateful Colombians named Bolívar President of their country, too, and before the end of the year he realized an old dream by combining the two countries into one, which he called the Republic of Gran Colombia.

In June 1821 Bolívar met and defeated a Spanish army at Carabobo, Venezuela. Now he was at last free to turn his attention to the struggle for freedom in the rest of South America. He made one more spectacular crossing of the Andes and marched into what is now Ecuador, planning to add it to his Gran Colombia. He also wrote a letter to José de San Martín, offering help in San Martín's struggle to liberate Peru.

While Bolívar had been fighting to free the northern tier of South American countries San Martín had been carrying on a parallel struggle in the south. In effect the forces of the two great generals were the claws of a giant pincer, both aimed at the ultimate stronghold of Spanish power in Peru —which had been the seat of viceregal authority and was still strongly royalist in sentiment.

Like Bolívar, San Martín was a military genius, but one of a wholly different kind. Where Bolívar was a brilliant tactician, San Martín was a sound strategist and a careful planner. The Venezuelan was flamboyant, the Argentine unostentatious and a man of unyielding rectitude. San Martín avoided political authority—which in those troubled times usually came with military success—as determinedly as Bolívar sought it.

San Martín's army showed the stamp of his careful, methodical nature. He took rough Gauchos, or cowboys, from the Argentine pampas and trained them to be smart grenadiers. When his highly disciplined troops were otherwise unemployed he required them to study mathematics. His idols were Napoleon and the Duke of Wellington, and he was said to keep a portrait of each flanking a matching portrait of himself in his quarters. If he did, it was his only flamboyant gesture; otherwise he was a modest man.

San Martín had first been sent by the newly independent Government of Buenos Aires to attack the royalist troops in Alto Peru (now Bolivia). He concluded that the royalist strength in Peru could never be crushed by way of the long, difficult overland route through Bolivia and the Andes. Instead, Chile must be liberated first; then Peru could be flanked by way of Chile.

The Argentine general set up a training base at the city of Mendoza, near the Chilean border. There he made preparations, as carefully as might the great Wellington, for an invasion through the towering Andes on the Chilean border. Uniforms, blankets, guns, ammunition, shoes for men and horses, slings for cannon and portable bridges to cross mountain chasms were manufactured on the spot.

At Mendoza San Martín was joined by the Chilean Bernardo O'Higgins, who had become leader of the revolutionary forces in his country. O'Higgins had fought brilliantly but unsuccessfully against a royalist army at Rancagua in 1814 and had been forced to flee the country with the remnants of his troops.

IN January 1817 San Martín, O'Higgins and their army were ready for their march through the Andes. Diversionary forces were sent through lower Andean passes to spread out the royalist units on the Chilean side. San Martín then led his main force through the highest passes of the entire Andean system, almost 20,000 feet in altitude and ice-clogged even at this time, the warmest of the South American year. He lost 5,000 mules, 1,000 horses and much equipment but got most of his men safely through.

In the first major engagement after the mountain crossing, O'Higgins led two dashing cavalry charges against royalist troops at Chacabuco and routed them. The Spaniards evacuated Santiago, and the town government offered San Martín the office of Supreme Director of Chile. San Martín, who said that he "came to liberate Chile, not to rule it," declined, and O'Higgins was made the head of the government.

There was one more major battle, at Maipú—another victory for the rebels. After that, Spanish power was ended in Chile except at a few isolated strongholds in the south. Under O'Higgins' leadership the new nation began assembling a fleet and recruiting forces for the liberation of Peru. O'Higgins exhausted Chile's meager resources and borrowed money from U.S. and British merchants. Lord Cochrane, an old British sea dog who had participated in Miranda's ill-fated attempt to liberate Venezuela in 1806, took charge of the growing fleet and added to it by capturing Spanish ships at sea. In a carnival air the fleet, consisting of eight warships and 16 transports loaded with troops and supplies, sailed out of Valparaiso in August 1820 bound for Peru.

SAN MARTÍN'S forces landed at Pisco a fortnight later and distributed handbills stating that their purpose was not conquest but the liberation of Peru and the consolidation of South America. San Martín delayed marching on Lima, hoping instead that the idea of liberty would spread in Peru and that Peruvians would flock to join his army. Finally, almost a year after the departure from Valparaiso, he sailed to Callao and marched into Lima. There he accepted the title of "Protector of Peru" and became, in effect, the first President of the country. But his forces were too weak to attempt a decisive battle with the royalists, who were making a strong stand in the country's interior. It was at this point that San Martín received Bolívar's offer of aid.

A meeting was arranged between San Martín, the liberator of the south, and Bolívar, the liberator of the north. Bolívar had marched down from Colombia, had won a battle at Pasto, and at Quito joined Antonio José de Sucre, his ablest officer, who had just overcome a large royalist army on the slopes of Mount Pichincha, above Quito. Bolívar was honored as a hero. There were processions, banquets and dances. He met Manuela Sáenz and began the love affair that would last to the end of his life. His plan for adding Ecuador to his Gran Colombia federation displeased some Ecuadorians, who would have preferred complete independence, but this did not diminish Bolívar's personal popularity.

The two liberators met at the coastal city of Guayaquil in July 1822. San Martín was 44, Bolívar 39. Both men were weary and ill, although Bolívar was buoyed up by his victories and honors while San Martín was somber and depressed. Both men were deeply concerned over the course of the independence movement. And they were right to be worried. The situation in Peru was precarious. Royalist forces were still strong, and the sentiment for independence was unreliable. San Martín, weary of political bickering, had begun to doubt the libertarian principles that had guided him earlier; he had even begun to think that Peru might best be governed as an independent monarchy. Peru needed Bolívar's help.

The two men talked alone. No record was kept of their conversation, one of the most important in the history of South America. Bolívar apparently promised aid, and San Martín is believed to have offered to serve under Bolívar's command. But after two days of talk San Martín secretly boarded his ship in the middle of the night and sailed back to Peru. He stayed in Lima only long enough to put down the disorders that had broken out in his absence. He then set sail for Chile, and his part in the liberation of South America was at an end—leaving the field to Bolívar.

WHEN Bolívar finally moved into Peru, joining Sucre, who had preceded him, he first had to restore order on the coast. While Peruvians were quarreling among themselves the Spaniards had reoccupied part of Lima for a time. Bolívar established control, however, and recruited new troops. Finally in 1824 he was ready to march from Trujillo, on the coast, into the highlands and meet the strong royalist forces holding out there. Bolívar reviewed his troops on the plain of Sacramento. Before him marched soldiers from Colombia, Venezuela, Chile, Argentina and, of course, Peru. The final effort was to be a truly international one.

Bolívar's international army had its first clash with the royalists at Junín, high on an intermontane plateau. It was a cavalry engagement in which horsemen fought with sabers and lances—with no gunfire. Infantrymen watched while Bolívar's horsemen drove off a large force of Spanish cavalry. But the decisive battle was not fought until four months later, in

December 1824, at Ayacucho. Here the revolutionary army of less than 6,000 men, led by Sucre, crushed a Spanish army of more than 9,000. Sucre forced the Spanish commanders to withdraw entirely from what is now Peru. Sucre then marched on into Alto Peru, defeated the last remnant of the Spanish forces in South America and helped establish the independent Republic of Bolívar, which was to become Bolivia.

BOLIVAR was at the climax of his career. The honors and titles that he loved so well were showered upon him. He was already Liberator and President of Gran Colombia (he had left the Vice President, Francisco de Paula Santander, in charge). Ecuador, which wanted to be independent of Gran Colombia, nevertheless wanted Bolívar as its President. He was for a time to be acting President of Bolivia. He was the first official President of Peru, was declared by the Peruvian congress to be the country's "Father and Savior," and was given by the Peruvians a Damascus sword set with 1,380 jewels and with a hilt topped by a liberty cap.

Bolívar was also acclaimed around the world. From the United States he received a locket containing a snippet of George Washington's hair. Lord Byron named a ship he had had built the *Bolívar*. Plans were under way for a congress to implement one of Bolívar's dreams: a federation of American republics. Even without the congress the recently liberated South American nations enjoyed, briefly, a greater unity than they had ever had as Spanish colonies or ever would have in the future as independent republics. The kinship of the Andean world under Bolívar's eccentric but brilliant leadership was the closest thing to solidarity since the days of the Inca Empire.

The various liberators, even before the sounds of battle had died away, began taking steps to cure some of the chronic injustices left over from Spanish rule. In Chile Bernardo O'Higgins opened up new lands and gave them to landless peasants. He initiated tax reforms and overhauled the judicial system. In Peru San Martín abolished serfdom and slavery, forbade forced labor, founded schools and a library, and decreed that "henceforth the aborigines shall not be called Indians; they are children and citizens of Peru and they shall be known as Peruvians." Bolívar freed slaves, established schools and distributed land to the Indians. These things were, of course, in addition to the establishment of governments, which, it was hoped, would function in countries unaccustomed to self-government.

But the governments and the idealistic reforms all came apart very quickly. Peru endured a rapid succession of military Presidents who believed in settling political matters with the sword. Peru tried, by invasion, to claim Ecuador, but the effort was thwarted by Peru's erstwhile "Father and Savior," Bolívar. Peru's internal affairs and international relations became progressively more chaotic.

BOLIVIA, after electing Sucre President, soon threw him out. Taking advantage of unsettled conditions in Peru, the Bolivians invaded their neighboring country and annexed it. Chile had a succession of *caudillos*, or military strongmen, and a civil war between liberal and conservative elements. Then, despite internal dissension, Chile went to war against the newly formed Bolivian-Peruvian federation— countries Chileans had fought to free.

Ecuador proclaimed itself independent and wrote a constitution of its own (the first of many). With this Bolívar's Gran Colombia disappeared, Venezuela also having withdrawn.

Confusion, even chaos for a time, is normal in the emergence of any new nation, but the Andean republics appeared to go far beyond the norm. There were many reasons. Spain had allowed the colonies no experience in governing themselves and had kept them isolated from a world that was changing rapidly, both economically and politically. In contrast to the situation in North America's British colonies, there had been no "legitimate" authority in the erstwhile Spanish colonies except for ineffectual town governments. In North America provincial legislatures had been authorized by the British Crown. When the authority of the Crown was destroyed in the American Revolution the provincial legislatures were ready to substitute the authority of the Continental Congress. There were no such legislatures in the South American colonies, no such authority and no logical transition to self-government.

When the revolution against Spain came it had a narrow base. It touched everyone, but the leaders were an intellectual and military minority. Peasants

and Indians were still not considered a part of society. Education among the Creoles who were to rule the countries was limited and knowledge of democratic ways almost nonexistent. The struggle for independence had developed military skills, but there was little political talent. There was virtually no middle class, no widely held body of public opinion, no familiarity with parliamentary procedures. When the first executives were chosen they were, naturally, the leaders in the wars of liberation —O'Higgins, San Martín, Bolívar, Sucre. Instead of being simply Presidents, they had grandiose titles and dictatorial powers handed to them. The first of them were, fortunately, high-minded and well meaning. But in most cases they were succeeded by men whose only qualification was military service. It was the beginning of a long succession of *caudillos* that was to afflict most of the Andean world; Chile alone among the four countries managed to free itself from the *caudillo* tradition early in its existence as a nation.

THE heroes of the great liberation all came to sad ends. O'Higgins was forced to resign as President of Chile and sought exile in Peru, where he spent the rest of his life. San Martín went back to Argentina, erected a tombstone on his young wife's grave and then went into voluntary exile in Europe. Sucre was killed by an assassin.

Bolívar worked furiously trying to hold his federation of Gran Colombia together but in 1830 gave up and headed for exile. He was penniless. His personal fortune had been spent in the wars, and he had refused the financial rewards that liberated countries had pressed on him. He was dying of tuberculosis. A few weeks before his lonely death in Santa Marta on the coast of Colombia he wrote a bitter postscript to his brilliant career: ". . . I have held power for twenty years and I have drawn but a few sure conclusions. America is ungovernable. He who serves a revolution ploughs the sea. The only thing one can do in America is to emigrate. This country will infallibly fall into the hands of an unbridled crowd of petty tyrants. . . . Devoured by all the crimes and extinguished by ferocity, we shall be disdained by the Europeans, who will not deign to conquer us. If it were possible for a part of the world to fall back into primitive chaos, America would."

Indian musicians in many-hued hats and heavy ponchos dance in procession and play flutes during the fiesta held in Puno, Peru.

Religious Festivals Punctuating the Andean Year

Religious celebrations, especially the annual holidays that blossom into gay fiestas, provide the Andean peoples with a necessary refuge from their hard lives and harsh environments. Some of the festivals commemorate Inca times; many more celebrate holy days of the Christian religion, which was imported and imposed on the area by the Spaniards. But all have a distinct, pungent flavor imparted to them by the Indians, who characteristically celebrate by wearing their gaudiest clothes, performing dances and drinking heroic amounts of native beer. The festivals commonly last for two or three days, the solemn religious observances quickly giving way to carnival. After the fiestas the exhausted revelers return to their long hours of work and their poor living conditions with little to look forward to but the next festival.

COSTUMED DANCERS dressed in the festival garb of their Andean town form part of the procession on Día del Puno, a fiesta held in Puno, Peru, on November 5, which celebrates the birth of Manco Capac and Mama Ocllo, the first Inca royalty.

REGAL BARGE carrying Indians playing the parts of Manco Capac and Mama Ocllo *(right)* emerges from a flotilla of skiffs on Lake Titicaca while derby-hatted Indian women watch. Inca legend held that these first rulers came from the lake.

Masked dancers perform the "diablada," or dance of the seven deadly sins, during the festivities.　　*Beaded strings are twirled by dancers in Puno*

*INDIAN FIESTA in
Peru re-enacts the birth
of the first great
Inca ruler and his Queen*

GALA DRESS adorns a young Indian lady at the Puno festival who has sat down to rest with a brightly colored handkerchief on her head. Her skirt of embroidered silk is the traditional *pollera* of the Aymara Indians, a tribe native to the Andes.

who march in front of the float bearing the Inca.

Fantastic feathered costumes adorn musicians who play panpipes and beat shallow wooden drums.

*CHRISTIAN RITES include an
elaborate procession in Lima
and a simple ceremony for the dead
that takes place in Cuzco*

SCATTERING INCENSE, a Lima crowd surges down a
narrow street *(above)* following a painting of Christ that
is carried through the city each November during the
festival of Our Lord of the Miracles, which began in 1747.

CARRYING THE PAINTING, purple-clad Limeños lead
the Lima festival procession *(left)*. The original painting,
which shows a dark-skinned Christ and is reputed to have
power to ward off earthquakes, was executed about 1651.

HONORING THE DEAD, mestizos from Cuzco, Peru,
visit a local cemetery *(opposite)* on November 2, which
is All Souls' Day. They place wreaths on the graves,
eat and drink, and leave gifts of food for the departed.

GUARD OF HONOR, playing flutes and drums, escorts the statue of the Virgin belonging to the village of Andacollo around the town plaza. Andacollo's fiesta falls on December 25.

CROWD OF WORSHIPERS takes Communion in the basilica of Andacollo, which was built with money collected from pilgrims who came to pray to the town's image of the Virgin.

GRATEFUL PILGRIMS enter Andacollo's church, many on their knees, to pray to the Virgin. Some 50,000 pilgrims a year seek to benefit from the statue's reputedly miraculous powers.

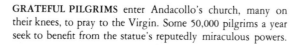

CHILEAN SHRINE *is the scene of a pilgrimage and fiesta honoring the Virgin*

Lima's splendid Plaza de Armas, laid out in 1535 by Francisco Pizarro, lies at the center of the Peruvian capital. Rising in contrast on

the hills beyond are the city's dismal slums, called "barriadas."

5

The Divided Nation

AT fiestas in some mountain villages in Peru a condor, the giant bird of the Andes, is trapped for the occasion. The condor's feet are tied to the back of a bull, and the bull is turned loose in the village plaza. The condor beats the bull's sides with its great wings and tears at the bull's flesh with its beak. The enraged bull charges into crowds of drunken, poncho-waving Indians who play at being matadors. Some of the Indians may be crippled, even killed. When the bull shows no more fight the condor is removed and *chicha*, a native beer, is poured down its throat. Then, to the accompaniment of a sorrowful Indian chant, the bird is released. If, despite the *chicha*, the condor can still fly and soars off into the mountains it is regarded as a good omen for the villagers.

Some folklorists say that this strange drama has traditional significance, that the bull is a symbol of the Spaniards, who introduced both bulls and bull-fighting to America, and that the condor, a native of the Andes, represents the Indians. If the folklorists are right this cruel spectacle is a dramatization of the

73

sharp division in the Andean regions between Indian and non-Indian elements, a division that began in the 16th Century with the Spanish conquest and persists today. The two worlds, of the white man and the Indian, are as unlike—and as antipathetic— as the condor and the bull, and have about as little to do with each other under normal circumstances. There are the obvious differences of language, diet, dress, education, manner, and the possession or lack of material goods and comforts. There are deeper differences of attitudes, beliefs and values that have never been reconciled.

Even the physical worlds in which they live are far apart and totally different. The coast and the lower valleys belong to the white man and the mestizo. The mountains and the *altiplanos*, or high plateaus, are the world of the Indian, although in a legal sense most of this vast area, too, belongs to the white man or mestizo. In Peru the capital of the white world is Lima, a bustling, pleasant city that sits on a desert littoral looking out to sea, its back to the rest of the country. The Indian capital—in a traditional, not political, sense—is the ancient city of Cuzco, nestled in a green and picturesque valley in the mountains, two vertical miles above sea level and 365 difficult horizontal miles from Lima.

BLOODY RITUAL of tying a condor to the back of a maddened bull occurs at fiesta time in a number of Andean villages.

Cuzco, when it was the center of the Inca Empire, was called *tahuantinsuyu*, the land of the four regions. Inca roads fanned out from it to the four regions of the old empire. Segments of these roads still exist. Much of Cuzco itself is built on Inca foundations. The walls of ancient Inca structures, solidly built of massive, carefully fitted stones, function as integral parts of colonial and modern buildings.

Past these buildings stream constant crowds of Indians. "There are not so many ants in Spain as there are Indians in this country," wrote one of the old Spanish chroniclers, and in Cuzco the same observation might be made today. There are tiny women in voluminous, earth-sweeping skirts, felt hats that in shape and decoration indicate the wearer's

place of origin, and shawls slung over the shoulders to carry a load of corn or wool or a sleeping infant. There are men in *chullos*, the distinctive Andean knitted caps with ear flaps. Their heads are thrust through ponchos woven in bright colors and patterns. The men carry huge loads of sacked potatoes, fruit, vegetables, grain, firewood or fodder. Or they may be driving strings of llamas laden with bundles of these same commodities. Children are dressed almost exactly like their parents. Their skins are deep bronze in color except for the cheeks which are usually chapped glowing red by the cold mountain wind and the brilliant sun. Almost all—adults and children—wear the *mueca de indio*, or Indian grin, in the presence of white men, a grimace that faintly resembles a smile but is not. Instead it is a defensive gesture against an alien world.

These people are descendants of the Incas. But unlike the Inca building stones, they have not been integrated into present-day Peru. They remain apart. Their feeling for the land and for the Indian community is much stronger than their allegiance to a vague entity called Peru which many of them still do not comprehend. Their links with the past are much stronger than with the present, and many of their customs and even religious observances look back to the centuries before the Spaniards arrived.

Many Indians, of course, do pay homage—heavily tinged with superstition—to the Christianity the Spaniards brought with them. A smoke-darkened figure of Christ in the Cuzco cathedral, which the Indians call *Taitacha Templores*, or Lord of the Earthquakes, is an object of special reverence. The fact that the model for the carving was a dying Spanish bandit does not impair its supposed powers. When, in 1650, Cuzco was almost destroyed by a series of earthquakes, the Indians prayed to the image and, being spared, made it the object of their most profound devotion. On Monday of Holy Week the figure, resting on a silver platform, is carried through the streets and pelted with *ñuccho*, an Andean wild flower. It is believed that during this procession a supernatural decision is made as to who will die during the year. The Indians fall to the pavement and pray that if it is their year to die they be granted the favor of a happy death.

The extraordinary reverence for religious objects of supposed miraculous virtues is one of the few links between the Indian society of the highlands and the white society of Lima. In Lima each October, there is a procession similar in spirit if not in appearance to that of Cuzco. For 16 hours a painting of the Lord of Miracles, also credited with supernatural powers against earthquakes, is carried through the streets with stately pomp by people wearing purple for the occasion. The Limeños throw flowers at this painting, just as do the Indians in Cuzco.

BUT such links between the Indian and non-Indian worlds of Peru are rare. From the very beginning, Lima and the Limeños seemed to be divorced from the rest of the country. Francisco Pizarro, conqueror of Peru and builder of Lima, turned away from the highlands and chose as a site for his colonial capital a place on the banks of the Rimac River, a short distance from the sea. Ships in the nearby harbor could carry the riches of the country back to Spain or, if need be, provide a ready escape.

Pizarro, proud of his rapid ascent from obscurity to the new aristocracy, gave his town the ringing name of City of the Kings, a name seldom used, however, since Pizarro's followers found it easier to call the settlement Lima, a corruption of Rimac. It was to become during the colonial era one of the world's most important cities, the viceregal capital of most of South America. Although separate viceregal capitals were later to be established in Bogotá and Buenos Aires, Lima remained the most important Spanish colonial outpost on the continent. Royalist tradition and sentiment were so dominant here that Peru, although the largest, was the last of the Andean countries to rise and fight for its independence.

In many places Lima still has the air of a colonial city. It can be sensed in the Plaza de Armas, flanked on one side by the cathedral, where Pizarro's remains are exposed to public view in a glass coffin, and by the national palace, where guardsmen wear plumed medieval helmets, high boots and sabers. It is found in the Torre Tagle Palace, which now houses the Peruvian Foreign Office, and in the hundreds of intricately carved, shuttered wooden balconies that overhang Lima's busy, narrow streets. There is a suggestion of colonial grandeur in the luxurious homes and gracious lives of the Peruvian aristocracy. Forty families are generally (and erroneously) believed to own all of Peru, but whether there are 40 or 400 it is true that most of the wealth is concentrated in the hands of relatively few families, and most of them live in Lima—when they are not in New York, London or Paris.

Great cities seldom reflect the character of their countries, and Lima does so less than most. Alexander von Humboldt, the explorer and naturalist who seldom went anywhere without learning something of interest or value, complained that in Lima he had learned nothing of Peru. And Peruvians themselves recognize that Lima bears little resemblance to the rest of the country and deplore the fact that most visitors see only the city and thus form a false notion of the nation's character.

Representative or not, Lima is an oasis of creature comforts, culture and commercial enterprise set down in a desolate landscape—an arid, sandy shelf between the mountains and the sea. For much of the year skies are gray. If Lima is not, as Herman Melville found it, "the strangest, saddest city thou can'st see," it is a somber one, in tones of gray, brown and dingy white, pleasantly relieved here and there by the brilliant colors of roses and geraniums. Its people are brisk, dignified and courteous—but they also are quick to flare up—violently, at times: a strike of bank clerks turns into street rioting; a dispute over an umpire's decision in a soccer game produces a panic in which hundreds lose their lives.

SOME faces display Indian features, just as some show traces of the Orient and Africa, and the mixture of bloods has produced a handsome people. The language is predominantly Spanish, but almost everything else displays an amazing diversity of origin. At a recent wedding uniting two of the most prominent and powerful families in Peru the list of the wedding party included such non-Spanish names as Garland, Ferrand, Heudebert, Saker, Griffiths, Hohagen and Fernandini. Many Peruvian aristocrats are fluent in French and English and speak them without an accent.

Some of the wealthy are, of course, descendants of the conquistadors and are indestructibly Spanish. Whether they are or not, families which have been wealthy for generations are regarded as *la oligarquía*. The oligarchy has traditionally owned most of the land of Peru—the cotton, sugar and rice plantations along the coast and the vast grazing lands in the sierra. Its members are singularly dependent upon the Indian population of Peru—and curiously detached from it. Indian servants staff their homes, cook and serve their food, and wait on them from infancy to old age. The aristocrats know these Indians and often treat them with kindness and affection. But the largest single segment of the Peruvian population is made up of *campesinos*, or serfs, who work on the haciendas, raising crops, caring for cattle and producing the country's wealth in a state of peonage. These Indians not only are unknown to the hacienda owners, but are as remote as the land itself.

DESPITE this social isolation Peru, for most of its life as a nation, has been governed either by the oligarchy or by the military which, traditionally, has represented the oligarchy. Such consistency, inequitable though it seems, might be expected to have produced an enduring stability. Strangely, it has not. Almost from the days of its birth as a free country Peru has been plagued with political uncertainty. Like other Spanish colonials, Peruvians were ill-prepared for self-government. Lima's moves toward independence were slow. The cry of independence was raised in La Paz on May 25, 1809, in Quito on August 10, 1809, and in Santiago on September 18, 1810. Independence was not declared in Lima until July 28, 1821. Part of the difficulty was, of course, that Spanish royalist forces were making their major effort in this, the most important colony of all. But in addition, Peru was not producing the kind of leadership needed for the struggle. There were no native patriot-soldiers such as San Martín, O'Higgins, Bolívar or Sucre. Peru's struggle for freedom was led by non-Peruvians.

But after the decisive battle against the Spaniards at Ayacucho in December 1824, Peru seemed to have military leaders in abundance, and for almost half a century they controlled the Government. A few of the old soldiers made good Presidents, notably Ramón Castilla, who dominated Peru from 1845 to 1867. Castilla established a Government monopoly of guano and with the proceeds serviced the public debt, built schools, roads and a telegraph system, abolished slavery and ordered an end to payment of tribute by Indians.

Manuel Pardo, Peru's first civilian President, took office in 1872 and governed well, but his administration established no pattern. In the years since then Peru has had almost as many military Governments as civilian, some of them duly elected but many taking office by coup. In 1962, when the military disagreed with the official returns in a presidential election, a junta representing the Army, Navy and Air Force again seized power. A Roman Catholic cardinal who protested the action was told by a member of the junta: "The prestige of the military is at stake."

The armed forces represent a constant in Peruvian political life—and also one of the major items in the national budget (18.4 per cent in the 1963 budget as compared with 22.7 per cent for education, 14.2 per cent for public works and development, 7 per cent for public health). The armed forces have, it is true, performed some useful nonmilitary functions for Peru—building roads and schools and educating illiterate conscripts.

BUT Peru's last need for a large military establishment was in the War of the Pacific, fought against Chile in the years 1879 to 1883. Since then military activity has been confined to border clashes with Ecuador. Peruvians find various explanations for the pre-eminence of the armed forces. One Peruvian historian observed that "while the *militares* inspired repugnance, the politicians inspired hatred." Another writer has said, "We continue to have a large army simply because we have a large army."

More often than not the military has been in league with the oligarchy, the large landholding and industrial interests. The alliance has been effective both in retarding social legislation and in inhibiting the development of broad-based, popular political parties. Despite this, Peru was the breeding ground of one of the most significant political movements in Latin American history, the Alianza Popular Revolucionaria Americana, better known as APRA. The party was organized by Víctor Raúl Haya de la Torre, a stocky, hook-nosed man who has spent much of his political life either in prison, in hiding or in exile. Haya was, in fact, in exile in Mexico in 1924 when he formulated the principles which have guided the party ever since and which have made it one of the most remarkable political organizations in Latin America.

In the Avenida Alfonso Ugarte in Lima, there stands a shabby onetime mansion that is now the Casa del Pueblo, or House of the People. It is the headquarters of APRA and a shrine to Haya. His books, his portraits and the bars from his prison cell are all prominently displayed. Here each night come crowds of workers, peasants and intellectuals for meetings on political strategy, for lectures on how to organize a cooperative, or for classes in reading and writing. They can receive instruction in art, music or even hairdressing, get free medical or dental attention, or, for a few pennies, get either a full meal or a haircut. It is the center of the most powerful political organization Peru has ever known but one that, strangely, has never managed to control the nation.

Haya was a student firebrand at the University of San Marcos in Lima during the regime of Augusto Leguía, an aristocrat who took power in 1919 with the support of the growing middle class and became the most absolute dictator of 20th Century Peru. Haya was deported, and while in exile he drew up APRA's five-point program. The movement is against imperialism, for the political unity of all of Latin America, for nationalization of land and industry, for the internationalization of the Panama Canal, and for the solidarity of all oppressed peoples and classes of the world. The program has Marxist overtones, and for a time Haya was courted by the

Communist world. But Haya insisted that the Russian formula would not fit Latin America and later declared that American imperialism was less to be feared than Communist imperialism. As a result both Haya and APRA have been as bitterly fought by the Communists as by the ultra-Rightists, and the two extremes have frequently allied themselves in opposition to APRA.

APRA has won some elections but has seldom exercised power. In 1931 the Apristas claimed that Haya had won the presidency, but since the votes were counted by friends of Colonel Luis M. Sánchez Cerro, who had recently resigned his dictatorial powers, the colonel was declared the victor. In 1936 an APRA-backed candidate for president won the election, but congress suspended tabulation of the votes and extended the term of President Oscar Benavides for three additional years. In 1945 a liberal President, José Luis Bustamante, was elected to the presidency with APRA support and Apristas took seats in the Cabinet and congress. But in 1948 APRA was outlawed once again, this time by the Apristas' friend Bustamante, and a few weeks later the Bustamante regime was overthrown by General Manuel Odría and replaced with a military Government under Odría's leadership. In 1962 Haya led the field of presidential candidates, but once more the military stepped in and annulled the election. After another period of government by military junta new elections were held, and a U.S.-educated architect, Fernando Belaúnde Terry, whom the military found acceptable, was elected.

Naturally, with its troubled history, APRA was usually combative and defensive on the rare occasions when it managed to wield legislative or administrative power, and its performance was therefore somewhat ineffectual. And since 1956, when it was

PERUVIANS PORTAGE A STEAMER

The first steamboat to navigate Lake Titicaca, the 138-mile-long highland lake that straddles the Peruvian-Bolivian border, was actually carried there on the backs of mules. Called the *Yaravi*, the steamer weighed 200 tons and was built in Scotland in 1862. That same year it was sailed under its own power from England to the southern Peruvian coast. There it was completely dismantled, and since the railroad to the lake was not completed, the pieces of the ship were portaged on muleback through some of the most rugged of all Andean country. At Puno, on the shore of the lake, it was reassembled with the greatest difficulty by Indian laborers under the direction of a dour Scottish engineer who knew neither Spanish nor any of the Indian languages. The *Yaravi* still sails the lake today, and has been joined by five other Peruvian steamships, the largest of which has a displacement of 2,000 tons.

most recently declared legal, the party has been preoccupied with maintaining its legality. As a result it has entered into strange alliances. The most recent one has been with ex-President General Odría, an old enemy and one of the many military men who had earlier driven APRA underground. APRA's leadership is aging, and it no longer has the appeal it once had for Peru's intellectuals. Nevertheless, it has had a great effect on Peruvian political life. Many APRA ideas have been taken up by others and put to work. Says an APRA leader: "APRA's ideas always go through three phases: First they say we are crazy; then they say we are Communist; then they say, 'What's new about this? It's what we've had in mind all the time.'" For example, the program of President Belaúnde's Acción Popular party, which came to power in 1963, bears many strong similarities to the program of APRA.

Had APRA's entire program of legislation ever been put into effect the result would have been a revolution, and this Peru has never had. Instead there has been a somewhat erratic evolutionary process in the direction of social justice, economic development, and integration of the country's human and material resources.

OFTEN this progress has been in the nature of an after-the-fact recognition of a problem that is solving itself, either badly or well. This is nowhere more apparent than in the *barriadas*, the shantytowns that surround several of Peru's large cities. Peruvian cities, like urban centers everywhere, are acutely short of housing. Miserable tenements and slum areas, already critically overcrowded, cannot accommodate the constant flow of population from country to city (at least half of Lima's two million people were born outside the city). These homeless persons—Indians and mestizos from the country and those crowded out of the city's tenements—have had to find their own solution. Their solution has been to form into groups and invade unoccupied land around the city. There, on barren hillsides or in dry riverbeds, they erect sprawling communities of shanties, the walls of the shanties made of straw mats held up by poles. Each squatter outlines his "lot" with stones, and the whole community bands together to resist the efforts of the police to evict them.

They organize rudimentary town governments and agitate for public services such as water, electricity and schools. When a squatter can he builds a brick or cement wall around his "lot," then builds interior walls and, finally, puts on a roof (not a prime necessity in an arid climate).

The *barriadas* have become cities in themselves. They were at first regarded as breeding grounds for crime as well as disease and as possible sources of revolutionary disorders. But it has become apparent that the *barriada* dwellers are, for the most part, solid, industrious people. After futile efforts to evict them the Government now makes it possible for them to acquire legal title to the land on which they have squatted illegally.

LUZ APAZA, 34, is a Lima *barriada* dweller. She is a native of the sierra in the Department of Ancash, and she faithfully goes back once a year to the principal fiesta in her native village. When she was still a child her mother died. She was brought to Lima by her father and lived with her sister in a straw shack in one of the older *barriadas*. She worked as a domestic, became skilled as a seamstress, and had two common-law husbands and a child by each. With the second husband she moved to the new *barriada* of San Martín de Porres. The husband disappeared, but Luz, with her earnings as a seamstress, built two rooms and a wall around the lot. She buys electricity from a neighbor who has a gasoline generator and carries water from a spigot 200 yards away. Luz and her two children still live in a mat-walled shanty at the rear. One of the finished rooms in front is rented. The other is a workroom where there are four old, foot-powered sewing machines (paid for on the installment plan) with which Luz and other women in the neighborhood turn out wholesale lots of simple children's clothes for sale in the markets.

Luz Apaza has title to her property and sometimes earns a little more money than she actually needs for current expenses. Her greatest worry is her older child, Jorge. He had an elementary-school education but was refused admission to a trade school because of the school's limited enrollment. He was turned down for enlistment in the Navy on physical grounds. He works in a factory for less than $30 a month, is defensive, sullen and pessimistic, and is a pro-Castro Communist.

The Peruvian Government is trying to stimulate the kind of development that will take care of the coming generations of Jorges. Opportunities for education and for industrial employment are being expanded. The rivers that drain the highlands are being harnessed to produce hydroelectric power. Old industries, such as mining, are being modernized. New industries, such as the production of fish meal (which increased almost 600 per cent in one recent 12-year period), are being encouraged. New roads are being built into hitherto inaccessible areas of the country where there are lands for development and resources for exploitation.

As a result of these and other advancements the urban areas of the country are changing rapidly. The sons of *obreros*, or laborers, are becoming *empleados*, or white-collar workers, and the sons of *empleados* are going to the universities. The urban middle class is getting bigger. Wealth and power, once tightly held by the owners of land and commercial enterprises, are spreading out among new industrialists, merchants and professional men.

One thing remains virtually unchanged in Peru: the status of the Indians.

In recent years the Government, through the Peruvian Institute of Indian Affairs, the Ministry of Education and other agencies, both Peruvian and foreign, has been trying to provide more education for the Indians, to train them in new skills and to encourage them to migrate to better land.

MOST widely known of all these ventures is the Cornell-Peru Project at Vicos, an ancient hacienda high in an Andean valley known as the Callejón de Huaylas. Here, beginning in 1952, Cornell University anthropologists and their Peruvian counterparts studied the needs of a backward Indian community, and, having done so, showed its members better ways of producing their major crop, potatoes. The anthropologists encouraged local initiative and leadership and guided the Vicosinos, eventually, in the negotiation for and purchase of the hacienda itself. Vicos has become a model Indian community, and the success of the Vicosinos offers encouragement to other Indians.

But such efforts are limited in effect to a small fraction of Peru's Indians, who make up almost half of the population and yet live outside both the political and economic life of the country. In 1964 the Government took a step long urged as the most basic need of the Indians: it passed an agrarian reform law. President Belaúnde had sent a draft of such legislation to congress within a fortnight of his inauguration. It took almost a year for the final law to be approved, but the urgent necessity of the measure finally drew together the most dissident political groups. The law will, hopefully, help to correct the imbalance in which 80 per cent of the nation's arable land is owned by a mere 1.4 per cent of the population while the Indians, who work the land, own little of it. The provisions of the new law specifically exclude agricultural or grazing lands which are being worked efficiently (and therefore contribute to the material well-being of the nation). Other properties will be subject to expropriation; the owners are to be paid by the Government in bonds and the lands given to the landless Peruvians (i.e., Indians) in units which are large enough to be farmed or grazed effectively.

WHETHER the law was passed soon enough remains to be seen. Before it was adopted the Indians, neglected and exploited for centuries, had begun direct action. Bloody uprisings by landless Indians have been frequent in recent years in all parts of the country but particularly in the highlands of southern Peru. Armed with little more than knives, sticks and a few old guns, Indian men, women and children have marched by the thousands onto private estates and occupied them, waving flags and banners and shouting *"Causachu el sindicato de campesinos"* (Long live the peasants' union). There have been a number of sharp clashes with soldiers and many deaths. In some cases, there has been clear evidence of Communist and other extreme Leftist inspiration, and several hundred alleged Communist agitators have been imprisoned. But the cause is older than Communism and older than Peru. When authorities try, peacefully, to make the land invaders desist, the Indians say, "What invasion? What we are doing is retaking the land of our ancestors. There are no invasions, only recoveries."

Trying to Realize
Peru's High Potential

Once the seat of Spanish wealth and power in South America, Peru is still the biggest and most populous Andean nation. It has a diverse and expanding economy and a strong potential for national prosperity. It also has problems: disparate geographic regions; a top-heavy wealth structure with resulting inequities; an uncertain political establishment plagued by an interfering military. The job that faces Peru's leaders is to keep the economy growing while seeing to it that the people get a fair share.

LIBERAL PRESIDENT, Fernando Belaúnde Terry looks over plans for new housing under a portrait of Colonel Bolognesi, a Peruvian hero. Belaúnde was elected following a 1962 coup.

INFLUENTIAL PUBLISHER, Pedro Beltrán, checking proofs in the composing room of his paper, *La Prensa,* not only is a journalistic power in Peru, but has been a Cabinet member.

REFORM LEADER, Víctor Raúl Haya de la Torre has been a center of political turmoil ever since he began fighting Peru's aristocratic leadership in 1923. He still leads his political party, known as APRA.

CHAMBER OF DEPUTIES, the 186-man lower house of Peru, convenes in Lima's Government Palace *(below).* Congressional power is limited; even the 55-man Senate can merely slow executive action.

COSMOPOLITAN LIMA *is the hub*
of Peru's social, cultural and business life

EXPENSIVE RESTAURANT, one of many in Lima, is patronized by members of the city's long-established aristocracy, which enjoys a position of unquestioned wealth and privilege.

FESTIVE GATHERING, called a *jarana*, is attended by a group of teachers at an informal restaurant in Lima. They are celebrating a special occasion with some food, drink and dancing.

TREE-LINED AVENUE in the wealthy Lima suburb of Magdalena frames a group of girls on their way to confirmation (*right*). Magdalena's mansions belong to Peruvian aristocrats.

BUSINESS LUNCH at the plush Hotel Crillon, involving U.S. and Latin American businessmen attending an economic conference, begins with the Peruvian cocktails called pisco sours.

EXECUTIVE COUNCIL of the University of San Marcos, which includes students and faculty members, meets in a handsome old chamber. San Marcos is South America's oldest university.

BAD HOUSING, *a chronic condition in Peru, gets worse as city slums spread*

SELF-HELP PROJECT gets under way in a Peruvian mountain town, where local workers use adobe bricks *(above)* to build a municipal building *(background)*. The Government provides tools and plans.

SLUM DWELLERS, a Lima family receives a visit *(left)* from their former priest, who is a member of the Compañía de Jesús, a Roman Catholic group that helps organize community centers and schools.

DESPONDENT SLOUGH of straw huts infests a hillside outside of Lima *(opposite)*. Some 400,000 Limeños live in *barriadas* like this or only slightly more permanent. All lack water, electricity and sewers.

THE DIVERSE ECONOMY of Peru,
*while gearing up for more industry,
still relies heavily on agriculture*

TINY FARM PLOTS nestle at the foot of a stark Andean cliff. Most of Peru's highland Indians are small-scale farmers who eke out a bare living by carefully tending small patches of soil.

SMELTING PLANT in the highland town of Oroya is part of the vast establishment of the Cerro de Pasco Corporation, Peru's biggest mining and mineral concern. The sign is an advertisement for sewing machines.

COTTON PLANTATIONS, such as the well-irrigated one opposite, produce Peru's largest export crop. Cotton also feeds a textile industry that employs more Peruvians than any other enterprise except farming.

MINING TOWN of Morococha *(right)*, in rich ore country 50 miles northeast of Lima, produces lead, copper, zinc and silver. Copper is the country's chief mineral export, roughly equal in value to cotton.

6

Latitude Zero

ECUADORIAN political orators, whatever the occasion, almost invariably emphasize two of their nation's claims to fame: first, that the Amazon was discovered by an Ecuadorian expedition; and second, that Ecuadorians were among the first to die for liberty in the South American struggle for independence. The claims have a touch of irony: the Amazon is very difficult to reach from Ecuador, and liberty has been rare for Ecuadorians.

The Amazon was, indeed, discovered by Spaniards who set out from Quito in 1540 to find "the land of cinnamon." Francisco de Orellana, a member of the expedition, discovered the river by mistake. Setting out in the expedition's boat to seek supplies, he was instead carried down into the vast river which came to be called the Amazon because of the "amazons" —fierce women warriors—whom de Orellana claimed he saw along its banks. This accidental voyage was the first descent of the Amazon to the Atlantic coast. But Ecuador, repeatedly victimized by boundary-jumping neighbors, has long since been cut off from approaches to the great waterway.

It is also true that Ecuadorian patriots were among the earliest and most vigorous pioneers in the movement for independence in the early 19th Century. But the liberty they proclaimed and fought and died for has remained elusive in Ecuadorian national life. The last day of Spanish tyranny, runs an Ecuadorian saying, was the first day of the new despotism. Much of Ecuador's life as a nation has been marked by bloodshed, dictatorships, territorial losses, natural disasters, civil strife and chronic Governmental instability. Executive power changed hands 67 times in the nation's first 133 years. For a president to serve a full term is counted a distinction. Only 13 have made it (and there once were four Presidents in the space of 26 days). Ecuadorians tell an apocryphal story about a newly arrived diplomat who presented his credentials to one president, received a formal call from the aide of another, and, his country having withdrawn its diplomatic recognition of Ecuador, said goodbye to a third, all in the space of 48 hours.

THIS political tumult goes on in a magnificent setting. Ecuador's scenery is as grand and tranquil as its politics are petty and feverish. The Andes, which in much of Peru, Bolivia and Chile are bleak and forbidding, here take on a rare beauty. The snow-covered peaks shine brilliantly in the equatorial sun. There is more rain than in the Andes to the south, and mountain slopes are checkerboards of green, with tiny Indian farm plots on the higher slopes and the vast fields and pastures of the great haciendas lower down. Mountain lakes are a sparkling blue where they are not covered with water hyacinths; lupine and wild fuchsia bloom along the roadsides. The nights are cold in the higher altitudes, but the days are like continual spring, the air sweet and fresh. Towns and cities nestle in the valleys and on the slopes, making pleasant patterns of tilted planes and tinted stucco among the cumulus clouds.

Beyond the mountains to the east is the Oriente territory, whose ill-defined boundaries have been and are a source of disputes between Ecuador and its neighbors, Colombia, Brazil and Peru. It is a jungle crossed by rivers that ultimately reach the Amazon and peopled with savages who pound out messages on drums, kill missionaries and shrink heads. It is a country possessing hardwoods, rubber, camphor, vanilla, sarsaparilla, ipecac (the source of an emetic), chicle, and what else no one knows, for it has never been entirely explored.

Between the Andean ranges and the Pacific lie more tropical lowlands. Where they have been cleared and reached by roads, there are plantations of bananas, sugar cane, cacao, coffee and rice. The coast, unlike the desert littoral of Peru and northern Chile, is lush and verdant. When you no longer see trees, say Ecuadorians, then you are in Peru. The nation's largest, most prosperous city, Guayaquil, is in the coastal lowlands. It has survived pillaging by pirates, bombardments by Peruvians, fires, the plague, yellow fever and malaria, and it has learned to build termite-proof buildings. It is a busy trading center. Its people are acquisitive, ambitious and distrustful of the highland capital of Quito. "We make the money," say the Guayaquileños, "and the Quiteños spend it."

Quito (as have most of Ecuador's highland cities) has suffered destructive earthquakes but has managed to preserve, in its older parts, a colonial air. There are ancient, beautiful churches, chapels and cloisters. The narrow, twisting Calle de la Ronda has changed little since the time of Sebastián Benalcázar, one of Pizarro's men who became the founder of colonial Quito. The 400-year-old hospital of San Juan de Dios is still in use, and the sound of old, well-tempered church bells is almost constant.

Ecuadorian historians and essayists like to say that Quito is the oldest national capital in South America. The city is no older, perhaps, than Cuzco, but Quito is still a capital and Cuzco is not. The site was the heart of the Quitu, or Quito, kingdom which was in existence for at least as long as the Inca Empire. Quiteños complain that the independent republic should have been given the romantic and time-honored name of Quito instead of being named for the equator. The people of Guayaquil, being anti-Quito, think the name "Ecuador" is fine.

NOT much is known of Ecuador's ancient Indian past. Comparatively little archeological investigation has been done, and many of the sites that a comprehensive study would need to uncover are forever out of reach, buried by volcanic eruptions and earthquake rubble. The different tribes worshiped various gods—the sun and moon, the volcanoes, a parrot, a huge emerald, a serpent and the sea. Many tribes excelled in ceramics and in the working of silver and gold. The Chibcha, Chimu, Quitu and Cara tribes were dominant in the area at various times. But all of them lacked both the social organization and the military techniques of the Inca Empire to the south, and they were finally subjugated and made part of the empire. One of the fiercest battles in pre-Columbian America was fought on the shores of Lake Yaguarcocha—the Lake of Blood—near the present city of Ibarra in Ecuador. Here Huayna Capac, father of the Ecuadorian-born Atahuallpa, whom the Spaniards executed at Cajamarca, fought the decisive battle in the pacification of Ecuador. According to legend, Huayna Capac killed 30,000 enemy Indians and dumped their bodies into the lake.

ALTHOUGH Ecuador in ancient times produced gold—and still produces some today—it was not as rich as several of the other countries the Spaniards conquered in South America. The expedition to the eastward that led to the accidental discovery of the Amazon revealed neither gold nor spices and was therefore regarded as of little consequence. Indian chieftains, such as the fearless Rumiñahui, who remains an Ecuadorian national hero, were tortured in an effort to find rumored—but apparently nonexistent—hoards of gold. Generations of Spaniards, and others since then, have sought vainly for the so-called Valverde treasure, named for an otherwise unknown Spanish soldier. Valverde was said to have been shown by his Indian father-in-law a gold-filled lake in eastern Ecuador. According to the legend, porters carrying a great treasure in gold (intended as part of the ransom of Atahuallpa) had reached this point when they heard that the Spaniards had killed their unfortunate ruler. Instead of continuing on to Cajamarca they dumped the gold into the lake. The secret of the lake's location died with Valverde.

Ecuador was administered first by the Viceroy of Peru in Lima, then by the Viceroy of Bogotá, again by Peru and still again by Bogotá, as if no one really cared. It had fine scenery and fertile soil, neither of which the Spaniards were seeking.

But Ecuador was far from quiet. Violence begins in this mountainous region with the earth itself. There were volcanic eruptions at the time of the Spanish invasion and again in 1575 and 1660. There were severe earthquakes in 1587, 1645, 1698 and 1797 (and more recent ones in 1868 and 1949, the latter killing 6,000 people). Communities in the earthquake belt have had to be rebuilt over and over again. Nor were the people quiet. The citizens of Quito rebelled in 1592 against a royal sales tax and again in 1765 over the rumor that rum dispensed by the royal monopoly was being poisoned in order to destroy the poorer classes. Both rebellions were bloody. The Indians rebelled against oppression in 1770, 1776 and 1790.

The spirit of rebellion was catching, and it became established among Ecuadorian Creoles (native-born whites) as well as among the mestizos and the Indians. Plotting for independence began as early as 1808, and a formal declaration of independence was made on August 10 of the following year. Many of the leaders of the movement were slaughtered in their jail cells less than a year later by royalist troops sent from Peru. By this time most Ecuadorians had become involved, and their struggle for independence became one of the fiercest in South America.

Although Ecuadorians revered Bolívar, their hero of the war was Bolívar's top general, the Venezuelan Antonio José de Sucre, the leader in the successful battle against the Spaniards on the slopes of Mount Pichincha, just outside Quito, on May 24, 1822. He was a brilliant soldier and one with a passion for justice. Had he not been assassinated by anti-Bolívar forces he might well have become president when Ecuador broke away from the Gran Colombia federation in 1830 to become an independent republic —and might have saved the country from much of the trouble that was to follow.

BUT instead another Venezuelan soldier, General Juan José Flores, became President and a prototype of the dictatorial *caudillos* who were to play an all-too-important role in Ecuador's subsequent history. Flores controlled the country for 15 years, surrounded by soldiers who treated Ecuador as though it were conquered territory. The feudalism that was characteristic of Spanish colonialism was perpetuated, and the development of free institutions was repressed. Even after Flores had been forced out chaos continued: there were invasions and blockades by Peru; some Ecuadorian provinces declared their independence and civil wars broke out. There were political groups that were described as conservative and liberal. Each group produced powerful *caudillos*, but regardless of the political label the end was always the same: violence and instability. It was not until the conservative Gabriel García Moreno came to power in 1861 that Ecuador began to make some progress.

Where Flores had relied on the Army for support, García Moreno, an almost fanatical Catholic, relied on the Church and governed with what might be called a religious despotism. Only Catholics could enjoy citizenship, and they were instructed to vote for García Moreno. He was dogmatic and dictatorial, but he achieved order, spurred foreign trade, and built schools and roads—as well as a stout prison. When García Moreno announced that he would seek a third term as President he was assassinated on the steps of the government palace in Quito. In a macabre ceremony his embalmed body, in dress uniform, with sword, plumed hat and sash of office, was seated in the presidential chair in the Quito cathedral for the funeral.

Ecuador's next effective President—20 years later—was a liberal, Eloy Alfaro, leader of an antifeudal, anti-Catholic movement that originated in the traditionally liberal coastal area. He and his liberal successor, Leonidas Plaza, took many steps frowned upon by the Church, such as the first divorce laws in South America and confiscation of Church estates. But Eloy Alfaro's greatest single achievement was the completion of the Guayaquil-Quito railroad begun by García Moreno. The railroad linked the two parts of the country that had until then regarded each other almost as foreign and unfriendly nations. Like García Moreno, Eloy Alfaro came to a grisly end: fighting broke out between factions of the Liberal Party and he was killed in jail, after which his body was dragged through Quito's streets, then dismembered and burned.

Ecuador's history, however, has not been entirely one of oppressive colonial policies and precarious independence. Quito was one of Spanish America's greatest centers of religious art; magnificent canvases and fine sculpture by mestizos and Indians were exported to all parts of the Spanish colonial world and filled Ecuadorian churches and cloisters to overflowing. An Indian, Manuel Chili, otherwise known as Caspicara (Pock-marked Face), carved lifelike figures of wood and painted them with a secret compound (said to include ox bile) that produced a porcelain-like finish. The most famous of the painters was Miguel de Santiago, around whose name many legends have grown up. One (also attributed to a Colombian painter) was that a student serving Santiago as a model for a painting of Christ on the Cross could not assume a genuinely agonized expression. Santiago seized a spear, fatally wounded the young man and then proceeded to paint authentic agony. Because of his crime—so the story goes—he took refuge in the monastery of San Agustín and remained there for 30 years. In any case, the walls of the old cloister are covered with paintings by Santiago and his students. Virtually all of Quito's old churches and monasteries are today treasure houses of colonial art. The Ecuadorian Andes were later to inspire many artists. Among them was Frederick E. Church, a U.S. painter of the Hudson River school which flourished in New York State in the mid-19th Century. After a visit to Ecuador, Church painted a gigantic canvas called *The Heart of the Andes,* which measures 5.5 feet by 10 feet and is now in the Metropolitan Museum of Art in New York City.

Because of its position, equidistant between the poles, and its variety of climate, Ecuador has also lured scientists, explorers and naturalists. The French Royal Academy of Science sent out an expedition headed by the great mathematician Charles Marie de La Condamine in 1735 to study earth measurements and to mark the position of the equator. Alexander

ECUADOR'S ODD AND DISTANT ISLES

Ecuador controls a large chain of islands called the Galápagos, which straddle the equator roughly 600 miles due west of the Ecuadorian mainland. Made up of five large islands and more than 70 islets and rocks, the Galápagos cover an area of 3,000 square miles. The islands were discovered in 1535 and for centuries were a refuge of pirates and whaling ships. More recently they have become a place of exciting discovery for naturalists, since the islands' animals, isolated from the mainland, have evolved some highly individual species. There are 500- to 600-pound turtles, and giant iguanas which grow three feet long and seem throwbacks to the reptilian age. Those monsters coexist with a species of penguin. The islands have been used as military bases, but little has been done to develop local industry and the human population totals only some 2,000.

von Humboldt, the German explorer and geographer, came to Ecuador, climbed the peaks of Pichincha and Chimborazo, and explored the headwaters of the Amazon. The observations of the British naturalist Charles Darwin in Ecuador's Galápagos Islands provided the foundation for his theories on the origin of species. The combination of high altitude and latitude zero creates favorable conditions for astronomical observation. Just outside of Quito, there is a satellite-tracking station; llamas graze on the lawn while scientists watch their space-age instruments.

BUT if the artistic and scientific accomplishments have been considerable, the marketable natural resources of Ecuador are few and peculiar. The country grows balsa, the featherweight wood out of which the Indians made huge rafts; vegetable ivory, which is used for buttons and carvings; *toquilla* fiber, from which "Panama" hats are made; cacao, source of cocoa and chocolate, a valuable but difficult crop, highly susceptible to disease; and several dozen different kinds of bananas, which since World War II have become Ecuador's principal export.

A few families have become wealthy from cacao —and usually have gone to live in Paris. But Ecuador has never had the huge family fortunes that have been characteristic of the other Andean republics. There were and are large landholdings, but in Ecuador a large landholding is measured in a few thousand acres as compared with hundreds of thousands elsewhere. Business and government tend to be controlled by a middle class, white and mestizo. One astute observer estimated recently that Ecuador is controlled by no more than 200 men, and of this number at least 90 per cent are distinctly middle class—some of them first-generation middle class.

As in Peru, almost half of the population is Indian, illiterate for the most part. The Indians, most of them living in the highlands on a bare subsistence basis, play almost no part in the nation's political or economic life. Some, like the remarkable Indians of Otavalo, are healthy, ambitious and, at least by Indian standards, prosperous. The Otavalo Indians are skilled weavers of ponchos, blankets and tweedlike suit materials. The men, scrupulously clean, in short white pants and with hair hanging down their backs in long braids, go as far afield as Colombia, Venezuela and Brazil selling their textiles. At home they use their earnings to buy more and better land which they cultivate profitably. In Cuenca the Indians have become hat weavers, and here again the handicraft has enabled them to buy land, livestock and farming equipment.

But too many of Ecuador's Indians live as *huasipungueros*. A *huasipungo* (literally, door of the house) is a small tract of land within a large hacienda. As elsewhere the Indian "belongs" to the hacienda. He is expected to work three or four days a week for the *patrón* for a few cents a day. He is given the use of a *huasipungo* on which to raise subsistence crops. The system is hopeless for the Indian and does nothing toward increasing productivity, which Ecuador needs. One solution may lie in colonization; many landless rural families are being moved from the highlands down into the fertile lowlands between the Andes and the sea. But it is doubtful whether new land can be made accessible fast enough to meet the country's needs.

WHEN Galo Plaza Lasso left the presidency of Ecuador in 1952, after one of the few stable and progressive administrations in the nation's history, he resolved to do something about the land-and-Indian problem. He returned to his 6,000-acre hacienda of Zuleta in the highlands near Quito (his mother's family have been landowners in Ecuador since the 16th Century). He knew the Indian *huasipungueros* of the hacienda and knew that, like all Indians, they tended to distrust any change, even a change for their own betterment. For this reason the first step had to be educational. He provided full elementary schooling for the children of the *huasipungueros* and offered scholarships for further education to those who showed promise. For the adults he provided classes in reading and writing and, what was more effective, paid a 20 per cent wage bonus to those adults who became literate.

Galo Plaza also provided a dispensary, free medical services, free toothbrushes and dentifrice for the children, and instruction in simple sanitation and hygiene. The *huasipungueros* were taught how to make their individual farming plots more productive. Finally, in 1964, when both the educational and economic level of the Indian community had been raised, Galo Plaza gave one fourth of the hacienda to the Indians who lived and worked there—180 parcels of land. A cooperative savings and loan association was established in which the Indians could save their surplus and from which they could borrow to build a modern, sanitary cottage or to buy a cow or an ox or a plow. Another cooperative was set up to market the embroidery and other Indian handicrafts. Work done for the hacienda is now optional —instead of compulsory as is usually the case—and it is paid for in wages far above the national average. The land owned directly by the hacienda has been diminished, but it is now worked efficiently by a dependable labor force, and there has been no loss in production. The Indian community, meanwhile, has become stable, healthy and independent.

A few other landowners have attempted to follow the Galo Plaza plan. In one case the landowner summoned his Indians and announced that he was giving each of them title to his *huasipungo*. The Indians, not having been prepared as they were at Zuleta, refused to accept the land, thinking that there must be some trick. The distrust built up through four centuries cannot be destroyed in one well-intentioned gesture. In some parts of Ecuador, notably in the province of Chimborazo, this distrust takes the form of open hostility to outsiders.

Ecuador has a new land reform law which may ultimately provide equitable distribution of land to the landless Indians, either through expropriation or through more intensive colonization of new lands. The new law also may stimulate more efficient and productive use of large private holdings.

LIKE many other recent reforms in Ecuador the agrarian law was not the result of normal legislative processes but of decree by a military junta. The military plays a disproportionately large role in the life of Ecuador. Incessant disputes over the country's boundaries (in the course of which Ecuador's national territory has been reduced from almost 270,000 square miles at the time of independence to about 110,000 square miles at present) have led to the maintenance of a large military establishment. In times of turmoil the military has invariably taken over the Government. Few Ecuadorians

like it, but there has seemed to be no alternative. Sometimes such military governments appear to get things done. The same junta that issued the decree for agrarian reform also took steps—still by decree —to tighten income tax laws and improve collection of taxes and customs, to establish a civil service and to modernize the nation's debt management.

WHY the dictatorial method has so often been necessary seems to baffle Ecuadorians—even the dictators themselves. Dr. José María Velasco Ibarra, a scholarly eccentric who has been in and out of the presidency of Ecuador since 1934—and a man who is never at a loss for words—says with unaccustomed brevity, "Ecuador is a very difficult country to govern." Another politician believes that all Ecuador needs is a new constitution (it has had 16). Still another has suggested that the solution may lie in the abolition not only of the presidency, but of the congress and the Army as well. Another shrugs and says, "Well, Ecuador still has the Virgin of Quinche [a statue revered in Ecuador as a protectress against earthquakes]. She will take care of us."

A U.S. political scientist, George I. Blanksten, made a study of Ecuador and traced *caudillismo*— the dictatorial rule of a *caudillo*, or leader—to the monarchic principles that guided both the Indians and the Spaniards. The hereditary precepts that had regulated both the Inca regime and the succession to the Spanish Crown were destroyed, the one by the Spanish conquest of Peru and the other by the war for independence in the early 19th Century. Ecuadorians, Blanksten concluded, lived "in the remnants of absolute monarchy which—shorn of the hereditary principle and containing no formalized system to replace it as a method of succession—they called a republic." The substitute for the monarch was usually a *caudillo*.

An eminent Ecuadorian historian, Alfredo Pareja Diezcanseco, says, "the dissatisfaction, hunger and hopelessness of the people are easily capitalized upon by any kind of demagoguery. The people want social justice. But, not having it, they believe they may find their salvation in the spectacular. . . . The liberty which the laws consecrate seems a deception. They love liberty as do no other people . . . but they suffer from hunger."

Barefoot and in country dress, Ecuadorian Indians look out of place as they walk around Independence Plaza in downtown Quito.

For Ecuador's Indians, a Slow Rise from Serfdom

Ecuador's most poignant social problem today is the future of the 88,000 Indian farm workers, the *huasipungueros*, who live in near-slavery on the great haciendas. Hampered by centuries of feudalism, the country's efforts at land reform are resisted not only by landowners but by many of the Indians, who distrust any change, good or bad. But land reform laws have been passed and machinery set in motion. Although progress is painfully slow a few enlightened experiments give glimpses of hope for the future.

THE HARD LOT of the "huasipunguero" is partly relieved by basic land reform measures

CROWDED QUARTERS are normal for *huasipungueros*. In this small thatched hut José Pilaguano, his wife María, his aunt and four young children live, according to María, "like little pigs."

PRIMITIVE TOOLS and a watchful foreman are the lot of the *huasipungueros* at right, who work their landowner's fields three to four days a week for an average daily wage of 37 cents.

MEAGER MEAL of boiled potatoes is the usual lunch for José and María Pilaguano. When not working for the hacienda they can farm a small patch of land lent them for their own use.

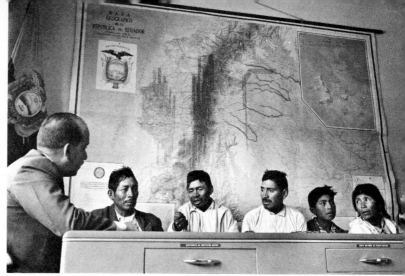

LOOKING FOR HELP, *huasipungueros* appear at a Government agrarian reform agency in Quito to ask that pressure be put on their landowner, who has not begun the required reforms.

TAKING STEPS to implement reforms, an agrarian reform agency lawyer *(right, foreground)* talks over the sharecroppers' complaints with an agronomist and the hacienda owner *(left)*.

GIVING AWAY LAND, the agency lawyer presents 68 Indians with titles to land ceded to them by another hacienda owner *(right, foreground)*. Each Indian got two acres and a house.

WORKING TOGETHER in a cooperative on the hacienda of Galo Plaza Lasso, Ecuador's former President, Indian women join forces to produce embroidery to sell to shops in Quito. They can also work in the hacienda's fields for proper wages.

KEEPING RECORDS of Galo Plaza's vast 6,000-acre hacienda, called Zuleta *(left),* is the job of Remberto Egas *(seated).* With him is Plaza's only son, Galo. In 1964 Plaza gave 1,600 acres of land outright to the *huasipungueros* living on his hacienda.

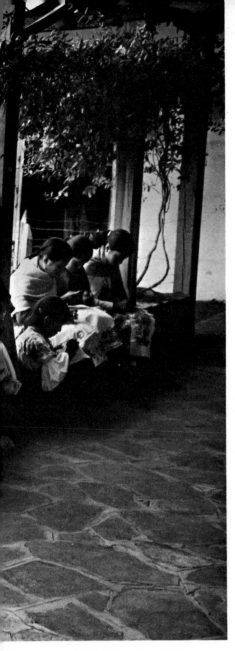

AT SCHOOL, built and administered by Plaza's hacienda, *huasipunguero* children *(right),* 200 all together, get a basic education. Adult Indians who learn to read and write are given a 20 per cent pay increase. The hacienda also provides medical care.

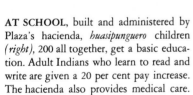

AT HOME, María Sandoval grinds corn for her family, using an age-old Indian method *(left).* The house, which belongs to the Sandovals, although Zuleta's managers helped build it, is much more substantial than most *huasipunguero* homes.

7

A High, Hard Country

IF revolution is taken to mean a change, usually abrupt, in the political power at the top, the Andean countries have had many such revolutions. But if revolution is understood to mean a deep, irrevocable alteration of a nation's political, economic and social character, of its institutions and its way of life, then only one of the Andean countries has undergone such a change: Bolivia. Since 1952, when the nation's old order was violently overthrown, Bolivia has been watched by its neighbors with a mixture of awe and admiration on the one hand and with considerable foreboding on the other.

The outward signs of revolution continue to be apparent in Bolivia. There are fresh flowers at the base of a lamppost where the body of a murdered President was displayed. Dissident politicians are arrested and sent into exile. The President's bullet-proof limousine is preceded by truckloads of soldiers as it sweeps through La Paz.

But the more meaningful marks of revolution are less obvious—subtle changes in the land itself, a high, hard country which Bolivia's reform-minded Government has been trying to make more productive, better adapted to meet the needs of a people who were for centuries among the most neglected in South America.

Bolivia is a remote land, locked in the heart of the South American continent. La Paz, the seat of the

A High, Hard Country

Government (the constitutional capital is Sucre, but only the Supreme Court is located there), and other principal cities are in one of the world's highest inhabited areas. Set in a valley in the heart of a bleak plain between 12,000 and 14,000 feet high, La Paz has blinding sunlight by day and nights that are bitterly cold and dark. The air is thin, without substance, and the stranger, his lungs laboring, has a feeling of vagueness and unreality. The whistling winds raise clouds of dun-colored dust in the dry season, and when it rains the gray clouds hang low, giving a feeling of oppressive gloom. The light tricks the eye: an adobe hut, a grazing llama or simply a rock miles away across the plain seems close at hand, and the ice-clad peak of Illimani looms threateningly over La Paz and seems even larger than it is. Where the torrents of the rainy season pour off the plateau, the brown-red earth has been cut into grotesque, lunar shapes.

THIS high, desolate area, the Altiplano, with its plateaus surrounded by towering mountains, is only a small part of the country, but it is the best-known part—and even it is little known to the outside world. When a 19th Century British emissary was insulted in La Paz, Queen Victoria is said to have ordered the British fleet to bombard the upstart country. Informed that this was geographically impossible, she ordered Bolivia, wherever it was, removed from the maps.

Victoria probably would not have believed it if she had been told that the Bolivian highlands were the home of a great pre-Inca civilization—a civilization that flourished even before there was an England. The stark stone ruins of Tiahuanaco, just south of Lake Titicaca, probably mark its center. Whoever these people were, they apparently came from the warmer lowlands to the east. They were an agricultural people, but some of their descendants became miners and smelters. They mined gold and silver, which they used solely for jewelry and decorations. Their most important gift to the conquering Incas, however, was bronze, shaped into weapons and tools and tempered almost to the hardness of iron. The Incas referred to these Indians as Collas, or people of the south, but today they are known as the Aymara, who, with the Quechua Indians,

make up the bulk of Bolivia's large Indian population. The Quechua, who were sent among the Aymara by the Incas, today outnumber the Aymara by about 3 to 2. The Aymara are somewhat taller and longer-limbed than the Quechua, and in disposition they are less gentle and submissive, more taciturn, stolid and suspicious.

Bolivia, which the Spaniards called Alto Peru (Upper Peru), was originally allotted to the ill-fated Diego de Almagro, whose land disputes with Francisco Pizarro, his onetime partner, led to much strife among the conquistadors. After Almagro's execution Francisco Pizarro sent his brother Gonzalo to pacify the natives. It was about this time that the Spaniards found the silver veins that were to be one of their most profitable discoveries in the New World. By 1545 the great "silver mountain" of Potosí was being exploited. The ores of Potosí, Porco and Oruro poured an unprecedented stream of wealth into the pockets of the conquerors and the treasury of Spain, and in the 17th Century Potosí became the largest city of the New World. It has been estimated that in the centuries since the Spanish conquest more than $200 billion in minerals has been extracted from Bolivian soil. Very little of the profits realized from the mines stayed in Bolivia, and in some ways the country was worse off for its mineral wealth. The Indians were dragooned into the mines; their carefully balanced agriculture, which under the Incas had made the sterile Bolivian highlands produce more than enough to feed their people, was disrupted.

THERE was resentment, not only on the part of the Indians, who existed as little better than slaves, but also among the Creoles, the native whites, who were discriminated against by colonial authorities, as they were in all of the Spanish colonies, the important positions being reserved for natives of Spain. Rebellions against the Spaniards began as early as 1661. In 1781 Indians besieged La Paz for nine months, and half the city's population either starved or was burned to death in fires started by flaming arrows and spears. In 1809 Bolivians were demanding freedom from Spain, and there was an unsuccessful revolt in La Paz led by Pedro Domingo Murillo, still one of the country's national heroes.

The last battle of the wars of independence was fought on Bolivian soil. Although the decisive battle had been fought at Ayacucho, Peru, in December 1824, Bolivia was not free until Antonio José de Sucre and his Colombian troops marched in and crushed the last royalist forces at Tumusla on April 2, 1825. The Bolivians declared their independence, named the country for Simón Bolívar, made him their first President (although he shortly transferred his executive authority to Sucre) and asked him to write their constitution. Despite Bolívar's avowed devotion to the republican system his constitution provided for a monarchic sort of president, one who would be elected for life and who would choose his own successor. The constitution was adopted in 1826, and Sucre was elected President. But he soon came to be resented as a "foreign dictator," and the 2,000 Colombian soldiers that he kept with him were regarded as a hateful occupying army. Finally he was forced out, and the new republic got off to an uncertain start. During its first troubled century Bolivia underwent 187 revolutions, rebellions and other political upheavals.

The best of Bolivia's early Presidents was Andrés Santa Cruz, son of a Spanish father and an Indian mother supposedly of pure Inca blood. He was Sucre's ablest aide, and he temporarily united Bolivia and Peru. He pushed the development of mining, agriculture and road building; however, the resistance of the Peruvians and armed intervention by Chile finally broke up the confederation. Santa Cruz was overthrown and went into European exile.

Of the many dictators the most bizarre was General Mariano Melgarejo, a black-bearded, amoral mestizo who led a revolution in the winter of 1864 to 1865 and ruled despotically until he was ejected by another revolution in 1871 (he was later murdered by the brother of one of his mistresses). His adventures with liquor and women were prodigious and his behavior as President and Commander in Chief incredible. Once when a foreign diplomat

ZANY STRONGMAN, General Mariano Melgarejo governed Bolivia with drunken illogic and an iron fist from 1865 to 1871.

complimented him on the iron discipline of his troops he was delighted and ordered a squadron of soldiers to march, on the double, out of a second-story window of the palace. He compelled officers to drink toasts to his prize horse, Holofernes, and at other times made them drop to the floor and "play dead" like dogs. He declared his birthday a movable feast, to be celebrated at the same time as Easter. When news of the Franco-Prussian War reached him he roared drunkenly for his troops to mobilize. He took his place at the head of the army and, his sense of world geography fuzzy at the best of times, started off to march overland to the aid of France.

Melgarejo might have continued indefinitely had not a heavy rain fallen, sobering him.

Like others, Melgarejo disregarded precedent, protocol and constitution. "I have put the constitution of 1861, which was very good, in this pocket," he is reported to have told an audience, "and that of 1868, which is even better . . . in this one, and nobody is going to rule Bolivia but me."

At the time of independence Bolivia consisted of 904,952 square miles of territory, including much of the mineral-rich Atacama Desert and approximately 200 miles of Pacific seacoast. It has since been reduced by more than 50 per cent through losses of territory to each of its five neighbors—Peru, Chile, Argentina, Paraguay and Brazil.

Bolivia's defeat by Chile in the War of the Pacific (1879-1883) very nearly wrecked the country economically. It was forced to give up its Pacific seacoast, including the port of Antofagasta, and its portion of the Atacama Desert, which proved to be of great value because of huge deposits of natural nitrate. Since that time Bolivia has existed as a landlocked country with no easy access to the outside world and has been afflicted with national claustrophobia. Twenty years after the War of the Pacific, in 1903, Bolivia gave up great potential wealth in natural rubber when it ceded the vast Acre territory to Brazil. But the most devastating misadventure, and one that was to have a profound effect on the future of Bolivia, was the 1932-1935 Chaco War with Paraguay. Paraguay had been severely beaten by the joint forces of Argentina, Brazil and Uruguay in the War of the Triple Alliance (1865-1870), so that Paraguay, like Bolivia—which was still rankled by its defeat by Chile—had suffered grievous injury to its national pride. Both countries were eager to avenge these defeats, and each had built up a new and well-drilled Army in the intervening years.

The war broke out over the Chaco, a vast and sparsely populated tropical plain, much of it unexplored, which lay between the two countries. No clear line of demarcation had ever been drawn. Bolivia based its claim on the administrative boundary of the Spanish colonial Government. Paraguay claimed much of the same territory on the basis of exploration and settlement. Bolivia's interest heightened after the loss of its seacoast to Chile; the Chaco could provide access to the navigable portion of the Paraguay River and hence a waterway to the Atlantic. The war might have been avoided by a cession of land by Bolivia and the granting of a port by Paraguay—and Bolivia's history might have been different. But despite some conciliatory gestures on the part of Bolivia both countries stood firm—their determination possibly strengthened by the discovery of petroleum in eastern Bolivia. There were repeated border skirmishes, an attempt at international arbitration and, finally, full-scale war in the wilderness of the Chaco.

Bolivia's Army, German-trained, was reputed to be one of the best in South America. The Paraguayan Army, made up largely of tough, resourceful Guarani Indians, was accustomed to the terrain, highly mobile and skilled at guerrilla tactics. Bolivia's troops

---

THE WORLD'S HIGHEST TIN MINES

Bolivia, which possesses some of the world's richest veins of tin, must mine its tin at higher altitudes than any other nation. The reason for this is the relative youth of the country's mountains. Beginning some 65 million years ago, when volcanic forces were creating the Cordillera Real, one of Bolivia's two Andean ranges, molten rock containing tin and other minerals, including silver, forced its way up through fissures in the Cordillera's granite mass. The result was rich veins of tin ore which, since the Cordillera has yet to suffer serious erosion, remain locked in the mountains' upper flanks. Elsewhere in the world many of the tin-bearing peaks have been eroded and much of their mineral wealth washed into valleys, where it lies in less concentrated but more accessible deposits. Despite the height of the Bolivian ore, tin was mined there as early as 1100 A.D. by Indians who used it in alloy to produce bronze. In modern times tin has become vital to manufacturing of all sorts, from toothpaste tubes to automobiles.

---

were largely Indian, too, but most of them were from the highlands, and in the Chaco they suffered from heat, tropical diseases and the change in altitude. Both Armies fought with heroism and the war ended with both sides exhausted, Bolivia having lost 60,000 men, Paraguay 40,000. By treaty most of the disputed territory was given to Paraguay.

The Chaco War was to be a seedbed of Bolivia's revolution. White officers became deeply concerned with the plight of their country. Indian soldiers, despite their hardships, had for the first time a sense of being Bolivians instead of simply Indians; they were never again to be as submissive as they had been in the past. A curious symptom of this change is the fact that the Indian troops, who on demobilization were given Western-style clothes, have never gone back to the traditional Indian garb they wore before the Chaco War took place.

The Government's official version of the effect of the Chaco War says: "The oligarchical governments of Bolivia had deceived the country as to its potential for war. In this moment of supreme need it did not have sufficient armaments, nor roads, nor means of transportation, nor efficient auxiliary services. . . . The Chaco War demonstrated that the oligarchy had sacrificed the most precious national interests at the service of the 'tin barons' who refused, in wartime, to pay taxes or deliver the foreign exchange needed for the national defense. . . . Thus was born, in war, a new national conscience."

The words "oligarchy" and "tin barons" were important in the Bolivian revolutionary jargon. Generally they referred to the old order and to established wealth, but particularly they were directed at the principal tin interests in Bolivia—the Patiño, Hochschild and Aramayo companies. Miserable working conditions in the tin mines (the life expectancy of miners was about 30 years), low wages and the glittering fortunes the owners piled up (and took abroad to spend) made the tin interests a natural target. Nationalization of the mines became a prime objective when the Movimiento Nacionalista Revolucionario (MNR) came into being.

The revolutionary movement that was fueled by the disasters of the Chaco War began to take shape during the regime of Colonel Germán Busch, a war hero who seized power in 1937 and was elected President in 1938. Under Busch's guidance a new constitution was written which, in addition to granting many social reforms, proclaimed the nation's ownership of all natural resources. Busch's plans for overhauling Bolivia led to charges that he was modeling his Government on that of Nazi Germany. The program was interrupted by his sudden death in 1939, a death which some of his followers claimed was murder but which was officially declared suicide.

Although Busch's program was short-lived it had several important results. The encouragement he had given to Bolivian workers, particularly the miners, led to riots at the Catavi tin mine in 1942. Government troops marched in and fired machine guns into the crowds of rebellious miners, killing 19 according to the official account, but probably killing many more. The massacre stirred resentment at repressive Government measures and was instrumental in spreading revolutionary sentiments.

Perhaps more important than the massacre was the organization of the MNR by followers of Busch, most of them intellectuals. Among them was a pale, intense economics professor, Víctor Paz Estenssoro—the most prominent and controversial figure of the revolution. Paz became a Minister in the Government of Major Gualberto Villarroel. The Villarroel regime, which took office in 1943, was bitterly opposed by the mine owners and came to an end in 1946 with a violent uprising in La Paz. Villarroel was shot in his office, and his body was dragged out and hung from a lamppost outside the Presidential Palace. Paz and other MNR leaders, who were in exile, plotted to recapture the Government. In the election of 1951 the MNR, with Paz as the presidential candidate, led at the polls but was prevented by the Army from taking power. As a result a revolution broke out on April 9 of the following year, 1952. The MNR was firmly allied with the labor movement; armed mineworkers overwhelmed the military, and within two days the old regime had been destroyed. Paz flew back from exile to take over the presidency.

The first order of business for the Revolutionary Government was to grant universal suffrage. Until that time the vote had been limited to adult males who were able to read and write Spanish and who had an assured, steady annual income. Simple as these requirements were they disenfranchised a large sector of the Bolivian population. The nation was about 60 to 70 per cent Indian; most of these were illiterate and very few had any income at all, since they lived by subsistence farming and bartering. At one stroke they were all made voting citizens of Bolivia—and, incidentally, a pillar of electoral strength for the MNR.

Three months later the Government nationalized the principal mines, the most important segment of the Bolivian economy. Although tin had been mined in Bolivia in pre-Inca times, it was neglected during the colonial era and during the 19th Century while the miners dug for more valuable silver and gold. But in the 20th Century Bolivia became one of the world's greatest tin-producing areas, second only to

THE GREATEST OF THE "TIN BARONS"

Of the several men who made vast fortunes in tin mining the most successful was a native of Bolivia named Simón I. Patiño. Born in 1862, Patiño in 1895 spent every penny he had to buy a small claim near the town of Oruro. The claim produced nothing but worthless rocks for four desperate years, although Patiño and his wife helped their Indian laborers dig with picks and shovels. Then, in 1899, a vein of tin appeared. Rushing to town to have a sample analyzed, Patiño found that he had hit a vein of 54 to 60 per cent pure tin, worth $500 a ton. By 1910 Patiño was wealthy, and the money continued to roll in until he became one of the world's five richest men. Patiño moved to Europe, where he lived like a rajah and became Bolivia's Minister to Spain and then to France. Despite his humble origins two of his children's marriages were sponsored by the King of Spain. He built railroads in Bolivia, banks to finance his operations and bought up mining operations the world over. During World War II he lived in a suite in New York's Waldorf-Astoria. He died in 1947, worth an estimated $300 to $500 million.

Southeast Asia. The following year, in 1953, Bolivia initiated an ambitious agrarian reform movement. The program was to be fraught with problems. Through the centuries Bolivia's Indian peoples had been basically agricultural. But the Indians' own efficient system of handling the land had been destroyed by the Spaniards. The Indians were pushed into smaller and less desirable tracts of land and made to work for large landowners under feudal conditions, and many had been forcibly removed from the land entirely and sent to work in the mines.

AFTER the Chaco War some Indian and mestizo *campesinos*, or peasants, had banded together in an effort to free themselves from feudalism. In some parts of the country, notably in the Department of Cochabamba, there were serious outbreaks of violence between the *campesinos* and landowners. A high-priority task for the Revolutionary Government when it came to power was to correct the injustices of land tenure, to satisfy the peasants' craving for land, to keep the peasant movement from going to political extremes, and somehow to raise agricultural production above the subsistence level— the kind of farming most familiar to peasants working small tracts of land, whether they owned them or not.

The Government's agrarian reform decree tried to meet all these requirements. All Bolivians of 18 or more years who wanted to farm were to be entitled to grants wherever land might be available. Large landholdings organized under the old feudal pattern were expropriated and the land divided into peasant homesites. Only those landowners who worked their own land and worked it efficiently, paying the *campesinos* decent wages, were to be allowed to keep part of their holdings.

The revolution proceeded on many fronts at once. The Army was disbanded. Miners and peasants were formed into militia units, and a new Army was formed around a cadre of officers who were in sympathy with the Government and its aims. Most of the rail lines were nationalized. Efforts were made to open up to colonization the vast areas of fertile lowlands in eastern and northern Bolivia which, because of a lack of roads, were isolated from the Altiplano, where the bulk of Bolivia's population had always

been concentrated. During the first 10 years of the revolution some 200,000 peasants moved from the higher areas into the lowlands. An ambitious program of school building and teacher training was launched to lower the staggering rate of illiteracy.

None of this was easy, and some problems were aggravated despite the revolutionary regime's good intentions. The Government's commitment to organized labor loaded the mine and railroad payrolls with nonproductive workers. Cars, locomotives and tracks of the nationalized railroads wore out, and the Government could not afford to replace them. Veins of tin ore began to be depleted, and there were not enough discoveries to make up the deficit in production. At a time when the world market price for tin was 80 cents a pound Bolivia was spending $1.03 to produce it. The peasants' newly won plots of land were not yielding the agricultural surpluses that the country needed. Educational progress was made, but it could hardly keep up with the increase in population (today there still are not enough schools for all of Bolivia's children). Per capita income began to increase—but it is still only a little more than $100 a year. Intrigues by Communists and Castroites have been a constant threat to the Government. Without foreign aid (the United States alone poured in more than $390 million in aid, loans and technical assistance in the first 13 years after the revolution) Bolivia's precarious progress would have ended in chaos.

BOLIVIANS know the dimensions of the task ahead of them. Government-owned mines and railroads are being overhauled, and efforts have been made to eliminate featherbedding. New techniques, seeds and equipment are being introduced to agriculture. The Indians, who have always been outside of the Bolivian social structure, are becoming part of it. The old saying that the Bolivian Indians' only modern possessions were the sewing machine and the chamber pot, one used and one not, is no longer true. Some Indians own bicycles and some own transistor radios, and they are at last becoming interested in a world which was a short time ago completely foreign to them.

Bolivia's best hope for the future lies in its wealth of comparatively undeveloped land to the north and east of the Altiplano. Where the highland areas lack water, fertile soil, fuel and even building materials, the lowlands seem to have everything in abundance —dependable rainfall, fertile land, hardwoods, fruit, vast pastures, and deposits of oil and natural gas. The principal stumbling block is, as it always has been, lack of transportation. While meat is scarce and expensive in the Altiplano, the plains of Mojos in the Department of Beni provide ideal range land and since the 18th Century have been thick with wild cattle, the result of pioneer stock-raising efforts by Jesuit priests. Yet for centuries the cattle were killed not for their meat but only for their hides. Because of the lack of transportation and refrigeration, there was no way of getting the meat to places where it was needed.

THE same lack of transportation for centuries almost completely isolated the eastern Bolivian city of Santa Cruz, an old Spanish settlement, from the rest of the country. The Santa Cruz area's abundant surpluses of sugar, rice and dried fruits could be carried to the Altiplano only by pack animals at great expense. When railroads were built in the early 20th Century connecting La Paz with the Pacific it became cheaper for the Altiplano cities to import these goods from abroad than to get them from Santa Cruz. Antipathies between the mining regions of western Bolivia and the agricultural areas of the east deepened, and there were groups in Santa Cruz that even threatened secession. But in 1954 the Government finally completed a road from the highland city of Cochabamba to Santa Cruz, and Santa Cruz became Bolivia's boom town, a center of agricultural and oil production.

It has, subsequently, also become the scene of one of Bolivia's most notable efforts to relocate its peoples. Colonies of Indians from the poverty-ridden Altiplano have been transplanted to the lowlands around Santa Cruz, as they have to the Alto Beni region north of La Paz and the Chaparé district near Cochabamba. Demobilized soldiers have been given tracts of newly opened land. Even foreign colonists have been made welcome (there are Italian and Okinawan colonies in the Santa Cruz area and also a settlement of the Mennonite sect).

Where there are roads, there has also been what might be called spontaneous colonization. Indians from the highlands, bundled in ponchos and wearing felt hats or wool caps, wander on foot down into the warm country. Many of them, never having seen trees before, become lost because the vegetation shuts out the sight of sun and stars. The food is strange—tropical fruits, unknown vegetables and meat—and it is abundant. The tools, such as machetes and axes, are unfamiliar and hard for the Indians to handle. Some of these wanderers cannot adapt to new ways and return to the harsh life of the highlands. But many of them stay, disproving the long-held belief that the Andean Indians will never willingly leave their ancestral home, no matter how inadequate it may be.

Some observers believe that the colonization movement can affect no more than an insignificant fraction of Bolivia's people, and that its chief value is as a safety valve for a troubled country. But Alfonso Gumucio Reyes, who as President Paz's Minister of Economy was a principal promoter of the Government's colonization plans, is convinced that the warm lowlands will in time be the dominant part of Bolivia in terms of population, wealth and resources. "In two generations," he says, "Bolivia will be a tropical country."

BOLIVIA has made encouraging progress in overcoming an environment that is perhaps more difficult and challenging than that of any of the other of the Andean republics. But it has not yet achieved the degree of political stability necessary for uninterrupted progress. In 1964 President Víctor Paz Estenssoro, just beginning his third elective term, was faced with a crisis largely resulting from his unsuccessful efforts to put the nationalized mines on a sound, economical basis. The new Army, which had been thought to be free of the power-seizing tendencies that had characterized its predecessor, turned against him. Paz was overthrown by a movement led by his Vice President, Air Force General René Barrientos. The immediate course of the national revolution in Bolivia may shift as a result of the coup. But the forces for change set in motion by the revolution will almost certainly continue to move inexorably toward the ultimate goal—rehabilitation of the long-repressed Indian population and development of the nation's economy.

New Leaders and a New National Force

Bolivian politics have always swayed to the vagaries of warring factions, but today's leaders have a new force to reckon with—the Indian. It was as a champion of Indian rights that Víctor Paz Estenssoro swept to power and began the far-reaching revolution of 1952. It was partly because of trouble with Indian tin miners that he was replaced by René Barrientos in the coup of November 1964. And it is with awareness of the Indians as a growing national force that the present Government pursues such programs as the improvement of working conditions and the opening of new land for settlement.

IMPRISONED STUDENTS who opposed President Paz and were freed after the coup in 1964 stand by their former cells amid papers scattered from their dossiers by other insurgents.

MILITARY RULER, René Barrientos *(center, opposite)*, the Air Force general who came to power after the 1964 turnover, listens to advisers beneath a portrait of Antonio José de Sucre.

DEPOSED PRESIDENT, Víctor Paz Estenssoro reads state papers *(left)* before his ouster in 1964. Paz was the leader of the political party which in 1952 started the reform movement.

TIN MINING, Bolivia's biggest business, makes punishing work for miners who live in bleak mining towns high in the Andes

ONE-ROOM APARTMENT houses miner Agustín Chile and his family of three in the Bolivian mining town of Caracoles. The furnishings include the family's only luxuries—two radios.

GRIM MINING TOWN of Caracoles, 150 miles from La Paz, looks dismal on a rainy afternoon as two miners walk home. Most of the miners at three-mile-high Caracoles are Indians.

MEDICAL CHECKUP is given at a mine dispensary to Agustín Chile *(below)*, who has tuberculosis. Many miners suffer from silicotuberculosis because they breathe so much rock dust.

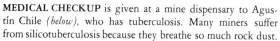

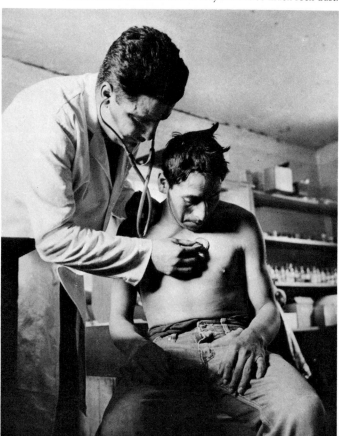

FILE OF WOMEN forms outside the commissary at Caràcoles (*below*), where mine families can buy food very cheaply. The store, part of a nationalized mine, is Government-subsidized.

SORTING THE ORE, the wives of Caracoles miners pick out rocks from a moving belt beneath paper fiesta decorations. The average monthly wage of all mineworkers is presently $102.

EXAMINING A SAMPLE, Indian miners discuss the quality of the ore. Decline in ore quality, old techniques, featherbedding and some bad management have put the tin industry in trouble.

AN EMERGING FORCE in Bolivia's national affairs, the Indian is gradually absorbing the ways of urban life

A SIGN OF THE TIMES, a Bolivian Indian family shops for a watch in a La Paz jewelry store. The Indians' increased buying power is a growing factor in the Bolivian economy.

EVIDENCE OF CHANGE, the Indian quarter of La Paz (*right, foreground*) is subtly taking on a more permanent appearance. Indians make up almost half of the city's population.

A MIXING OF WORLDS occurs in the downtown streets of La Paz, where Indian women wearing their traditional full skirts and bowler-style felt hats gather to sell their handmade goods. Many still come to the city just for the day or for a while during the farming off-season, but increasingly the Indians are leaving their highland farms and moving to new areas.

armers ever since the Incas terraced the hillsides

FERTILE OASIS in the usually hostile highlands, Lake Titicaca provides water and a pleasant climate. The terraces in the foreground were originally built by the Incas to combat erosion.

RED-ROOFED TOWN of Copacabana, near Lake Titicaca, has been a goal of Indian pilgrimages for centuries. It remained a shrine even after Christianity replaced the Indians' old religion.

STONY HILLSIDES like the one below make farming in the Altiplano difficult. Most Indians, though they own land under the new laws, can wring only a bare subsistence from the soil.

LOWLAND FARM AREAS are opened up by Indians in Government colonizing projects

PRIMEVAL FOREST still covers most of the Yapacaní area's 200,000 acres *(left)* near the Bolivian Andes' eastern slopes, where farmland is slowly being cleared.

NEW SETTLER in the Yapacaní area, Antonio Lara *(above, right)* goes home after a day spent clearing the forest. The Government gave Lara 30 hectares (75 acres).

FARM LUNCH brings together Lara's family *(below)*, which includes a wife and eight sons. They have cleared a portion of their land and have planted some crops.

The Uttermost Land

SIMON BOLIVAR, who had never been there, once admiringly described Chile as "that uttermost part of the earth," and predicted future greatness because of its isolation from "the vices of ancient Europe and Asia."

Whatever the reason, Chile, separated from the rest of the world by deserts, ice-clad mountains, oceans and Antarctica, is a country distinct not only from its Andean neighbors to the north but from all the rest of the American republics as well.

The very shape of the country is distinctive: a long, multicolored ribbon of land stretching 2,600 miles from the tropics to Cape Horn. Some parts, such as the Central Valley, are fertile and highly productive, with grainfields, orchards and vineyards. But to the north, there is barren desert, and to the south, where there is heavy rainfall, dense forests share the rocky land with glacial lakes. The land ends in a cold archipelago, a region of storms, high winds and wild ocean. Chilean place names, given here in translation, are a catalogue of travail: Hill of Anguish, Last Hope Sound, Dead Mules, Ice Water Valley, Horse-Eating Pass, Gulf of Sorrows.

The people are as varied and full of contradictions as is the landscape. Writers, seeking an analogy, have described them as South American Yankees or Englishmen or Germans. None of the comparisons is either accurate or flattering to a people of strong national feeling. Chile is a melting-pot country, no more Spanish than the United States today is English. Spanish names are mingled with those of English, Irish, Scottish, German, Basque, Slavic, Italian and even Arabian origin. "He who sets foot on Chilean soil is free," says the national constitution. It might well have added "and Chilean," for whatever their origin the newcomers take on a complicated set of characteristics that are peculiarly Chilean.

THEY are a people of pride and self-confidence and wear both well, whether they are members of the aristocratic Union Club in Santiago or stevedores in Valparaiso. Chileans are good-natured and easygoing. But they are also bad enemies with little regard for life—their own or that of others. They dress with style and dignity, yet the national folk hero is the *roto,* or ragged man, a swaggering, reckless, fast-talking, freelance laborer. They are inordinately proud of their country's military history and of the excellence of the armed forces, yet theirs is one of the few nations on the continent in which the military is subservient to civilian government. They are race-conscious and speak of being a "white" country, but boast in their national hymn of having Indian blood—as many of them do. They are highly sensitive to *categoría,* or status, yet they are among the few Latin Americans who can and do laugh at themselves. There is a definite aristocracy, but there is also one of the most advanced systems of social welfare for nonaristocrats. At the same time, there are grave ills in the social and economic order which seem at times to outrace the lawmakers and their laws. Chileans revere their orderly political processes but joke about their politics and their politicians. Possibly as a result of this the politicians, for their part, behave with restraint and tend to avoid pomp, ostentation and bombast.

They are intemperate in some things. The late Ludwig Bemelmans, the humorous writer, told of a would-be journalist who had failed in his effort to launch an afternoon newspaper in Santiago because, the frustrated man said, by afternoon Chileans were so full of wine they could not read. The tale is suspect since there are a number of lively and widely read afternoon newspapers, but Chileans do drink such large quantities of their fine wine that there is

little left to export. They are also addicted to gambling, to living beyond their means, to sports and to dancing the *cueca,* a highly suggestive folk dance. But whether drinking, dancing, gambling or simply going about their business, they are great respecters of law and order, and their Governmental institutions are famous for their soundness.

Chileans are seldom evasive or secretive and usually speak with an un-Latin directness. Their women are less bound by obsolete social codes than are other Latin women and are generally regarded as among the Western Hemisphere's most agreeable and charming. John "Foul Weather Jack" Byron, grandfather of the poet Lord Byron, was, as a young sailor, shipwrecked in Chile. He found both Chile and the Chilenas delightful: "Fine sparkling eyes, ready wit, a great deal of good nature and a strong disposition to gallantry." His observations have been repeatedly seconded by later travelers.

Chileans are both literate and literary. They are a people with a passion for history, and it used to be said that an educated man became either a lawyer or a historian or both. Some historians, such as Benjamín Vicuña Mackenna, rank as national heroes. The late Nobel laureate Gabriela Mistral is seldom referred to simply as "the poet Mistral" or as "Señorita Mistral," but almost always as *"la divina Gabriela,"* even in casual conversation.

THERE is also a taste for literary irreverence. *Topaze,* a magazine of political satire, won a worldwide reputation under the editorship of Jorge Delano. The best-selling book in recent Chilean literary history is a slim, little paperback called *Revolución en Chile,* a sly commentary on Chile's complicated politics. The book was supposedly written by a British woman journalist named Sillie Utternut. Miss Utternut, the creation of two Chilean journalists, Guillermo Blanco and Carlos Ruiz-Tagle, finds everything in Chile "picturesque and enigmatic," interprets abusive Chilean slang as flattery, mistakes drunken parties for Indian uprisings and firmly believes that revolution is just around the corner.

Chile has had its share of revolutions and political upheavals, but its life, first as a Spanish colony and later as a nation, has followed a more even course than have those of other Andean republics. One of

Chile's advantages is geographical. Where the other Andean nations are divided by the Andes, Chile is in fact unified by them. There is little of the regionalism that produces distrust and misunderstanding between Quito and Guayaquil, La Paz and Santa Cruz, or Lima and the rest of Peru.

The past is no burden to the Chileans. There are no monuments to a pre-Hispanic past, such as Peru's Machu Picchu or Bolivia's Tiahuanaco, and, thanks to recurrent and destructive earthquakes, few relics of the Spanish colonial era. The native Indians, the Araucanians, built no great cities, but were instead hunters and fierce, ingenious warriors. But they were never very numerous and today number no more than a few hundred thousand—a tiny minority in a population of more than eight million. Traces of Indian ancestry are apparent in many faces, but Indians and Indianism do not shape Chilean economics, politics or culture.

THE Chileans' debt to the Spaniards is almost as slight. The pessimism, stilted manners and obsessive piety of the Spaniards are all alien to Chile. Chileans have a strong sense of tradition, but it is a Chilean tradition, one that they have developed themselves.

Chile's connection with Spain even in the colonial era was tenuous. Lima, seat of the Spanish viceroy, was far away, and Spain was much farther. Diego de Almagro, Pizarro's original partner in the conquest of Peru, was given Chile as a sort of consolation prize. Almagro made a tentative exploration of the country but, finding little gold or silver, withdrew. Pizarro next sent a formidable warrior, Pedro de Valdivia, to conquer Chile. Valdivia founded the capital, Santiago, in 1541 and wrote a letter to his King saying ". . . this land is such that there is none better in the world." Valdivia was correct in one sense; he had found a temperate climate and fertile soil. But Chile was not the country of wealth and allurement that Peru was; it had no Indian palaces, no cities of stone, no treasure, no romance —and it did have the fierce Araucanians, who destroyed buildings and fortifications almost as fast as the Spaniards could put them up. Everyone had to fight, including Valdivia's mistress, Inés de Suárez, who personally led the defense of Santiago against an Indian attack one time when Valdivia was away. Valdivia himself was killed in a later battle against the Araucanians.

Geographically remote, dangerous and seemingly poor in resources, Chile was treated as an inferior colony. Where more important parts of the Spanish empire were administered by *audiencias,* governing bodies second in authority only to the viceroy, Chile was left in the charge of a captain-general. The Chileans' principal contact with Peru and Spain was by means of ships which, bound to or from Europe by way of Cape Horn, stopped in Chilean ports for provisions. Most Chileans worked on the land and in their isolation became tough, self-reliant and more independent than other Spanish colonists.

Bernardo O'Higgins, the principal fighter for Chilean independence, was also the first governor of an independent Chile. Far more than either San Martín or Bolívar, O'Higgins was deeply committed to the ideals of representative government and democracy. But the times were not favorable to either, and he governed as the "Supreme Director." Nevertheless, O'Higgins established schools, founded a library, paved streets, and installed lighting and sanitation systems in Santiago. He forbade Chileans to use titles or coats of arms. He also tried to foster a new class of small farmers and at the same time attempted to do away with the *mayorazgos,* or large landholdings. This brought him into open conflict with the *hacendados,* the landowners. The landowners joined with the clergy and forced O'Higgins to abdicate and go into exile in Peru, where he died without ever again seeing the country that he had freed.

TURMOIL followed O'Higgins' departure. There were clashes between liberals, impatient for political and social change, and the conservative landowners. The landed interests finally won; the constitution written in 1833 reflected their dominance and preserved oligarchic authority in Chile for nearly a century. The constitution withheld the right to vote from those who were illiterate and those who had neither property nor regular income—thus denying the franchise to a great majority of Chileans. The voting requirements were later eased, but the control by the *hacendados* continued. Chileans long complained that their Government had four branches—the executive, the legislature, the judiciary and the National Agricultural Society.

The man most responsible for enactment of the 1833 constitution was a portly merchant named Diego Portales, a sort of Chilean Alexander Hamilton. He never rose above ministerial rank, but he nonetheless wielded great power. He insisted that Chile must have a strong central government in the hands of aristocrats in order that the "citizens can be led along the path of order and virtue. . . ." Once this had been achieved, Portales felt, it would be time to think about democratic government. He straightened out the young country's finances and established the tradition of civilian control over the military. He also bears responsibility for Chile's first war with Peru and Bolivia, but, assassinated by mutinous troops, he did not live to see the outcome.

Chile went to war twice with Peru and Bolivia, first in the years 1836 to 1839 to crush the Peruvian-Bolivian Confederation, and again 40 years later in the War of the Pacific, or the "Nitrate War" (1879-1883). The latter was fought over the ill-defined country called the Atacama Desert that then constituted western Bolivia, southern Peru and northern Chile.

Except for a few mines and the guano found along the coast this was wasteland and would perhaps have remained so but for the discovery of unsuspected riches. There was an abundance of a saltlike substance in the desert that the Spaniards called saltpeter and used only for the manufacture of gunpowder and fireworks. That it was a powerful natural fertilizer was discovered, it is said, by accident. Prospectors had noticed that the white rocks around their campfire sometimes sputtered with flames. One of them took a sample to a priest, thinking the flames might be a manifestation of evil. The priest analyzed the material as sodium nitrate, and having done so threw the sample out into his garden, where, in short

DARWIN LOOKS AT SOUTHERN CHILE

Besides providing evidence for his theories of evolution, Charles Darwin's voyage on H.M.S. *Beagle* from 1831 to 1836 gave him a chance to report observantly on many parts of the world, including the forbidding southern coast of Chile. The following excerpts are from the *Voyage of the Beagle*.

Several glaciers descended in a winding course . . . to the seacoast: they may be likened to great frozen Niagaras . . . a little farther northward there are so many breakers that the sea is called the Milky Way. One sight of such a coast is enough to make a landsman dream for a week about shipwrecks, peril and death.

Great masses of ice frequently fall from these icy cliffs [the glaciers], and the crash reverberates like the broadside of a man-of-war, through the lonely channels.

order, his flowers and vegetables began to grow in an unprecedented fashion. This tale may not be true, but however the discovery was made, there was soon a large demand for nitrate fertilizer. Chileans and foreign investors were eager to make the most of it, and they began mining nitrate on Bolivian territory. Discovery of the rich silver mines of Caracoles in 1870 heightened Chile's interest in acquiring larger holdings in the Atacama Desert.

Bolivia was at first disposed to make concessions to Chile, but then broke a promise not to increase the duty on nitrate exports. Chile thereupon seized the ports of Antofagasta, Cobija and Tocopilla. Bolivia declared war and was soon joined by Peru. It was a disastrous conflict for both countries. Bolivia lost valuable mineral resources and its access to the sea. Peru lost the province of Tarapacá, and Lima suffered a ruinous and humiliating two-year occupation by Chilean troops.

The European demand for the nitrates Chile now controlled brought the country wealth and fame. Dusty desert settlements became bustling frontier towns. Nitrate ships crowded the ports of northern Chile. Export taxes on nitrates were the principal support of the Chilean economy. The boom continued until World War I, when German scientists perfected a means of producing synthetic nitrate to replace the imported natural nitrate that had been cut off by the war.

It was then and is now a peculiarity of the Chilean economy that it tends to be based on one exportable product and that the exploitation of that product is largely in the hands of foreigners. The most prominent figure in the nitrate era was a flamboyant Englishman, "Colonel" John Thomas North, who mined and sold nitrates, built railroads and shipping lines, meddled in Chilean politics and foreign policy, and accumulated one of the world's great fortunes.

Other fortunes were made in copper, which had been mined and smelted by Indians in what is now Chile long before the Spaniards arrived. Even before the War of the Pacific—which greatly increased Chile's copper-producing capacity—Chile was mining nearly 40 per cent of the world's copper supply. The boom in nitrates eclipsed copper for a time, but in the 20th Century, copper again assumed the commanding position in the Chilean economy. As was the case with nitrates the dominant interests were foreign—American this time. William Braden, an engineer, acquired the El Teniente mine in central Chile in 1904, and the Guggenheim interests bought the great Chuquicamata mine northeast of Antofagasta in 1912. Braden's company later became a subsidiary of Kennecott, and the Guggenheim holdings were sold to Anaconda. Ninety per cent of Chile's copper production remains in American hands (Anaconda alone is responsible for half of the production). Mineral exports, principally copper, account for more than four fifths of Chile's export earnings, while taxes paid by the mining companies make up more than half of Chile's revenue.

DEPENDENCE on copper has made Chile's economy lopsided. Copper is a perennial political issue and conditions Chilean thinking on many subjects. The people even calculate values in terms of copper. "We once were able to buy an American automobile with a ton and a half of copper," a Santiago industrialist said recently. "Now it takes three tons." A drop of one cent per pound in the world price of copper can mean a loss of $15 million a year to Chile. The nation's dependence on copper has led to much agitation for nationalization of the industry. Finally, late in 1964, President Eduardo Frei reached a tentative agreement with the Anaconda and Kennecott companies under which the American copper interests would increase production, refine more of their output in Chile and turn over to the Government some stock in their Chilean affiliates. In return for these concessions the Government would give assurances against tax increases and nationalization of the copper mines.

The mining industry has affected Chilean society as well as the economy. Chile was traditionally an agricultural country with a small amount of arable land tightly concentrated in a few hands. Those who did not own land worked for those who did. *Inquilinos,* or tenants, were, in an almost feudal sense, dependent upon the *patrón* for everything—food, clothing, protection. If they were allowed to vote at all they voted as the *patrón* wished. The mines and the industries gave Chile an independent working class and, later, a middle class. These groups first challenged and then broke the close political control the landowners had exercised for so long.

THE first indications of a changing order began to appear during the administration of José Manuel Balmaceda (1886-1891). Chile was at the height of its nitrate boom but was suffering—as it has suffered almost ever since—from inflation. Balmaceda came from a wealthy family but had the instincts of a reformer and a set of pronounced liberal ideas which appealed to the country's workers and its emerging middle class. Unfortunately he also had the instincts and manners of a dictator. He gave great impetus to public education and imposed higher taxes on the wealthy—thus arousing the fears of landowners and the rest of the oligarchy. He talked of nationalizing the nitrate properties—thus crossing swords with "Colonel" North, the "Nitrate King." Eventually the Chilean congress, weary of Balmaceda's ironhanded regime, allied itself with the Chilean Navy and began a rebellion. The ensuing civil war cost 10,000 lives. Balmaceda committed suicide on the last day of his term.

Despite this setback the political strength of the working and middle classes continued to grow steadily in the years after the civil war. It reached political effectiveness in 1920, when Arturo Alessandri, the candidate of the Liberal Alliance, became President. Laws passed under the Alessandri regime placed Chile among the most progressive countries of the world in social legislation. A code guaranteeing protection and rights for labor, social security laws, separation of church and state, and a new and liberal constitution all came under Alessandri's presidency. The almost complete political control exercised by the landowners was finally ended.

But the new laws and constitution—and much legislation since—have not kept up with Chile's mounting social and economic problems. Although the political power of the landowners has been reduced, archaic systems of land tenure and use endure. Fewer than 10 per cent of the landowners control 86 per cent of the arable land. Little of it is used efficiently, and Chile's food imports have been growing steadily for the past 20 years. Rural families make up a third of the population, but most of them exist in a state of hopeless poverty. Their urban cousins are little better off. Real wages have declined disastrously in recent years. The lower half of the population gets only 15 per cent of the national income and is chronically undernourished and inadequately housed. More than three fourths of working-class families live in only one room, usually in squatter settlements.

Further industrialization is badly needed to reduce Chile's unhealthy reliance on mineral exports as the principal support of the economy and to supply goods for which Chile now pays out precious foreign exchange. And it would inevitably provide more jobs. But the greatest barrier to such increased industrialization is the lack of a mass market for industrial products.

COMPLICATING the dilemma is Chile's notorious monetary inflation. Prices began spiraling in a period of prosperity immediately after the War of the Pacific, and except for a few years during the Depression of the 1930s they have continued to do so ever since. In the decade from 1940 to 1950 prices rose 412 per cent, and in the following decade a monstrous 2,089 per cent. Chileans on fixed wages and salaries are cruelly victimized. Some public servants with important positions are forced to get by on one meal a day; others support their families by holding down one or more "moonlighting" jobs. For those who manage to live on their incomes, there is no incentive to save for the future.

The hardships resulting from the inflationary process have had political consequences. Far-Left political parties draw strength from the laboring class, but they also have made substantial gains in the middle class, normally a bulwark against the Left. In the 1958 presidential election Jorge Alessandri, a conservative, won by the narrow margin of 30,000 votes over Salvador Allende, a Marxist backed by the Socialist and Communist Parties. Six years later,

there was no Conservative candidate in the field, and Allende appeared to be even stronger than before. His principal opponent was Eduardo Frei, a Christian Democrat. It was clear that the gravity of Chile's economic ills was generally recognized; the program of the Christian Democrats was only a little less radical than that of the extreme Left.

In the final stages of the 1964 Chilean presidential campaign, there was heightened interest in Chilean politics in many world capitals—of the East as well as the West. It appeared that a Communist-backed candidate might win the presidency of one of the most important nations of the Western Hemisphere in a free election. Santiago was full of rumors of wealthy Chileans exporting their fortunes to "safe" countries and booking airplane seats for the day after the election. A Santiago lawyer scoffed at such nervousness. "Certainly we have many defects in our economic system," he said, "and there are many grave social injustices. But we are Chileans and in time we will attend to these things, no matter who wins the election. What others do not understand about us is our feeling for laws. . . . Where else do you find street vendors selling copies of the latest laws, shouting *'Una ley para hoy, señor'* [A law for today, sir], and people buying them eagerly? Our laws are stronger than buildings."

"Our geography may be crazy," said a Santiago newspaper editor, "but our history is sane and sensible." Such firm expressions of faith in Chile's ability to survive and, ultimately, thrive in a world full of uncertainty seemed to be borne out by the 1964 election which the world watched with such apprehension. It was calm and orderly, and Frei, the Christian Democrat, won decisively over the candidate backed by the extreme Left.

RIGHTLY or wrongly, many Chileans insist that it would not have mattered who won the election because in the end the Chilean passion for legality and order would prevail. In the main they agree with Bolívar's prediction: "Chile is ordained by its natural situation, by the simple customs of its virtuous inhabitants, to enjoy the prosperity proportioned by the just and sweet laws of a republic. If any republic is to last a long time in America I think it will be that of Chile . . . Chile can be free."

Painted brightly and terraced to capture the sun, apartments near Valparaiso are frequently rented by Chileans for the summer season.

The Contrasting Climate of Confidence in Chile

To go from the northern Andean countries into Chile is to move not only into a new geographical zone but into a completely different political and social climate as well. Chile has many of the serious problems that bother its northern neighbors and has even added a few of its own, such as the staggering inflation that has plagued the economy for more than 60 years. The big difference is that the Chileans are blessed with national unity and political stability and seem to be prepared to solve their difficulties by peaceful, legislative means. Thus armed, they move ahead confidently, working industriously in their mines and vineyards, playing vigorously on their beaches and coping earnestly with their problems.

125

SEASIDE RESORTS, crowded with enthusiastic, hard-playing Chileans, dot a spectacular coastline

SOAKING UP SUN on the beach at Viña del Mar, five miles from Valparaiso, beachgoers take advantage of Chile's temperate summer weather, at its best from December to February.

ENJOYING THE SCENERY is part of the attraction of Viña del Mar *(left)*, which also boasts a casino and the President's summer retreat. It is one of South America's most popular resorts.

RELAXING IN COMFORT, Chilean painter Pablo Burchard Jr. *(below, center)* entertains on summer weekends at his home in Zapallar, an exclusive resort on the coast north of Viña del Mar.

GIGANTIC OPEN PIT, the Chuquicamata mine in northern Chile, two miles long and 1,200 feet deep, is the world's largest copper mine. Chile ranks third in copper production, after the U.S. and Russia.

HUGE FLOCK of sheep *(opposite)* is rounded up by mounted shepherds on a farm in southern Chile, where a cold, wet climate forces the sheep to grow a thick, heavy wool that is Chile's biggest nonmineral export.

LONG ROWS of grapevines *(right)* stretch to the hills on the Estación Santa Ana near Santiago. The vineyard, run by the Undurrago family, is the most famous of the 32,000 vineyards in Chile's Central Valley.

REFORM-MINDED LEADERS *have won popular support for welfare programs like Government housing*

LANDSLIDE WINNER, President Eduardo Frei *(above, far left)* chats with advisers after a television talk. Frei was elected in September 1964 with the biggest plurality in Chile's history. His Christian Democrat platform calls for broad social and economic reform.

FUND-RAISING DINNER in Santiago *(below)* pushes the candidacy of Christian Democrat Rafael Gumucio, who went on to win a seat in the Chilean Senate in March 1965. In the same election President Frei won a 56 per cent majority in the Chamber of Deputies.

MIDDLE-INCOME HOUSING is provided for workers by a Government-sponsored project in Santiago. Chile first passed housing legislation as early as 1906, but decent housing for a rapidly expanding and urbanizing population remains a major national problem.

HOMEMADE HOUSE is built by Javier de Alamos and his family *(right)* in a project called San Gregorio in Santiago. The Government provides wooden bricks and other materials and gives Alamos 21 years to pay. There are about 4,000 units in the project.

A POETRY LECTURE at Lima's ancient University of San Marcos is delivered by Gerardo Diego, poet, professor and member of Spain's Royal Academy. Professor Diego spoke on the work of the Peruvian poet César Vallejo, who died in 1938.

9

A Cultural Quest

DIFFERENT in many ways, the Andean countries are alike in the intensity of their creative and intellectual life which, more often than not, reveals great pride in the remarkable past and a deep and militant concern with the troubled present.

There is high respect for the arts and a wide participation in them. A lawyer will confess that he is also a poet and a Government functionary that he is a writer of historical essays. To be sure, writers and artists complain, as they do everywhere, of the meagerness of the market for their work. One Peruvian novelist has said that "in Peru no one reads books—the poor because they are illiterate and the rich because they are indolent and stupid"; and a Bolivian painter has complained that "there isn't a decent art gallery in all of Bolivia. . . ."

Nevertheless, the visitor is impressed with the number of thriving bookstores in the principal cities, with the crowds at concerts, with the number of people in museums and at art exhibitions, and with the encouragement the Governments give to serious intellectual and artistic pursuits through such institutions as the remarkable Casa de la Cultura, or House of Culture, in Quito, Ecuador, which is a combination publishing house, museum, art gallery, lecture hall and dispenser of Government grants.

But with all this high enthusiasm for culture, there are at least two elements which render the Andean cultural scene complex. One is the close tie between politics and the arts. Painters and writers who have steered clear of political currents are the exception. Fernando Belaúnde Terry was an architect before he turned to politics and became President of Peru. Peru's best-known novelist, Ciro Alegría, no longer publishes very much because he is too busy being a member of the Chamber of Deputies. Many artistic groups have broken into vocal, warring schisms over Castro, Communism and the perennial bugaboo, "Yankee imperialism." Political militancy has even been fostered by the grants and scholarships given by various Cold War competitors, and it is a rare writer, painter or student who has not been offered a free trip to the U.S., Europe, Moscow, Havana or Peking.

A SECOND element that makes the area's arts rather difficult to comprehend and categorize is a multiplicity of cultural heritages. First there were the highly developed Indian civilizations which held sway in most parts of the Andean world for a thousand years or more. Then there was Spanish colonialism, which controlled the life, destiny and thoughts of the Andean nations for three centuries. Finally, there was the struggle for independence, a struggle which in a cultural sense is still going on today.

The latter two stages in this progression were marked by efforts to eliminate traces of the immediately preceding stage. Through the centuries before the Spaniards came, there had been a gradual evolution of social institutions and artistic sensibilities. That which was best in each period seemed to survive, whether in stone carving, ceramics, architecture, weaving, city planning, metallurgy, religious worship or instruction of the young. The culminating Inca civilization was adaptive rather than creative, an impressive amalgamation and refinement of everything that had gone before.

But the Spaniards did their best to destroy all traces of the Indians' achievements. Pedro de Cieza de León, a good soldier and an honest amateur historian who went to Peru in 1547, lamented: ". . . it is a sad thing to reflect that these idol-worshiping Incas should have had such wisdom . . . and that we, Christians, have destroyed so many kingdoms. For wherever the Spaniards have passed, conquering and

discovering, it is as though a fire had gone, destroying everything in its path."

The invaders razed temples and cities, broke or burned (or melted into bullion) all accessible examples of the highly developed Indian arts, and disrupted the intricate but efficient social organization—and for all this they substituted alien European forms and patterns. That the Indian peoples survived, deprived of the heritage that made them great, was due less to the Spaniards' humanity than to their need for slave labor.

The rebels of the early 19th Century were just as eager to wipe out the marks of Spanish oppression as the Spaniards had been to get rid of the artifacts of a sophisticated heathenism. But the rebels were at a disadvantage. Their knowledge, their instincts, and their powers of reasoning and of expression had been shaped by the very people they sought to overthrow. Spanish officers and Spanish soldiers might disappear. Spanish institutions and characteristics— arbitrary government, a rigidly stratified society and feudal concepts of property—endured, as did Spanish and other European cultural values. The thinkers and writers and teachers who helped foment the fight for independence thought and wrote and taught as Spaniards, the only distinguishing feature being their passion for political and economic liberty.

THESE passions were strong, and these thinkers, writers and teachers played an important role in the creation of a continent of new nations. Francisco Eugenio de Santa Cruz y Espejo, a doctor who became a brilliant essayist and the founder of Ecuador's first newspaper, is regarded as the father of his nation. He was jailed in 1795 for his libertarian beliefs and died before the struggle for independence began, but his writings circulated from hand to hand and helped launch the fight for freedom in Ecuador. One of the most eminent Ecuadorian figures in the war for independence was a poet, José Joaquín de Olmedo, who wrote much heroic verse about the struggle.

In Peru the intellectual preparation for independence was as strong as the political capabilities were weak. With the first university and the first printing press on the continent, Lima had been the cultural as well as the administrative center of the South

American colonies. Late in the 18th Century a number of intellectuals, among them Hipólito Unanue, Isidoro de Celis, José Banquijano y Carrillo, Toribio Rodríguez de Mendoza and Diego Cisneros, organized the Society of Friends of the Country and published a journal, the *Mercurio Peruano*, to enlighten the public in economic and political matters and to lead the way to freedom. In Bolivia similar services were rendered by Vicente Pazoz Kanki, a journalist and historian, and José Manuel Loza, a poet who also wrote on politics and philosophy.

INDEPENDENCE, once achieved, might have brought with it freedom of thought and expression, a liberation from the tight Spanish-European mold and the development of a truly native culture. But Spanish domination was followed in most of the nations by a succession of native despots, and the oppression was worse than before. The best creative efforts were now directed against dictatorships and injustices, and the style was, of necessity, still polemic. The spirit of dispute, of controversy and criticism became the most marked characteristic of Andean literature and to a large degree has remained so ever since.

Of the various polemics that helped shape the modern Andean world, among the most bitter—and least known elsewhere—were those directed against the Ecuadorian dictator Gabriel García Moreno, who was a political power from 1861 to 1875, by a slender, hot-eyed mestizo writer named Juan Montalvo. Montalvo railed against the dictator who had "divided the Ecuadorian people into three equal parts: one dedicated to death, another to exile, and the last to servitude." And he harangued the public for submitting to despotism: "Officious, noisy, squabbling people, who lie, prattle and bray like donkeys without reason; rude, brawling, selfish people; useless, cold, crumbling people; little, sly, whining people...." Punishment for the dictator, Montalvo wrote, "is ripening in the womb of Providence." In his pamphlet *"La dictadura perpetua"* (The Perpetual Dictatorship) he helped create the climate of violence which finally destroyed García Moreno. After the dictator had been assassinated on the steps of the national palace, Montalvo is popularly supposed to have boasted, "My pen has killed him."

Montalvo necessarily spent much of his life in exile, and he died in France. Exile was normal for literary men who wrote in the Montalvo manner and for many who did not. Even the great Peruvian 19th Century traditionalist Ricardo Palma, whose specialty was writing charming, irreverent and non-political tales, spent part of his career in exile. Chile alone among the Andean countries has been comparatively tolerant of militant writers and has often served as a refuge for writers exiled from its neighboring countries.

Neither exile nor repression discouraged these belligerent intellectuals, and national disasters fanned their creative fires. Peru's defeat by Chile in the War of the Pacific, for example, stimulated much critical writing by Peruvians, and their influence can still be traced in that country's modern intellectual currents. Most important of the disillusioned Peruvian writers was Manuel González Prada, who had served in the war and who had been angered by Peru's ruinous defeat and by the nation's inherent weaknesses which made such a catastrophe possible. He was violently anticlerical and pro-Indian and insisted that the guilt for Peru's plight lay with the Church, the military and the oligarchy. His famous injunction—"Old men to the tomb, young men to action"—became a rallying cry for generations of liberals.

AMONG them was José Carlos Mariátegui, a brilliant thinker and writer who was strongly influenced by Marxism and became the founder of the Socialist Party of Peru. But the philosophy that he developed in his *Seven Interpretive Essays on Peruvian Reality* was more Peruvian than Marxist. Before he died in 1930 at the age of 35 he had laid down certain lines of thought that were to influence greatly the evolution of political and intellectual life in Peru. He held that there must be a new kind of Socialism based on American concepts—such as the Inca system of communal landownership—instead of on European industrialism, as Marxism was; that education must not be restricted to the children of the wealthy and aristocratic, but must be made available to all, white and Indian alike; and that there must be an alliance between peasants and workers.

In Bolivia, too, the most brilliant writers scorned purely literary pursuits and poured their energies into denunciations of political and social injustice. Alcides Arguedas, a diplomat and writer, criticized both Bolivia and Bolivians: everything in his country, he complained, "is immense—everything except man." While he had sympathy and admiration for the Indians, he felt that they were doomed, and he deplored the society that a mixture of Spanish and Indian blood had created. "Out of the fecundating embrace of the white race and the Indian," he wrote, "comes forth . . . [the] *mestizo,* bringing as an inheritance the characteristic traits of both: from the Spaniard the belligerent spirit, his introspectiveness, pride, vanity, accentuated individualism . . . and from the Indian his submission to the strong and powerful, lack of initiative, resignation in the face of all evils . . . ." Another Bolivian diplomat and writer, the mestizo poet Franz Tamayo, who died in 1956, was also critical of Bolivian society and government, but he had faith that the Bolivian people would create a great nation once a social system had evolved fitted to their talents and capacities.

The concern with Indians and with Indian problems found in Arguedas and Tamayo is one aspect of *indigenismo,* roughly translatable as "Indianism," which for much of the 20th Century has been one of the strongest single influences in the arts and literature of the Andean world. The Indians' grand and mysterious past, their sufferings in the conquest, the richness of both pre-Columbian arts and contemporary folk arts, and the misery and hopelessness of the present-day Indians have all provided material for generations of writers and artists.

THE interest in Indians is not new. As early as 1569 a talented Spanish soldier named Alonso de Ercilla published in Spain the first part of his long epic poem, *La Araucana,* which tells of the Spaniards' battles with the indomitable Araucanians in Chile. Ercilla had written his poem on scraps of paper, leather and wood while in the field. The style was European, but the poem was a ringing glorification of the New World savages. Chilean schoolchildren today know many of the poem's cantos by heart. There was also a colorful and none-too-accurate chronicle of the Inca past written by Garcilaso de la Vega, son of a Spanish soldier and an Inca Princess. Garcilaso's history provided a mine

of picturesque material not only for historians but for novelists, dramatists and essayists.

The Indianism of Ercilla and Garcilaso was essentially romantic. The Indianism that has become a powerful force in the intellectual life of the Andean countries in the 20th Century is intensely realistic, based on the current plight of the Indians. Probably the most widely known novels of the region—*Huasipungo* by the Ecuadorian writer Jorge Icaza and *Broad and Alien Is the World* by the Peruvian novelist Ciro Alegría—deal with the Indians' attachment to the land and their exploitation by white landowners. The poetry of Peru's César Vallejo and the prose of Bolivia's José María Arguedas show a strong concern for the unhappy lot of the Indians.

IN painting and sculpture, Indianism represents a rebellion against the sterility and conformity of colonial art. Colonialism in the arts had persisted for nearly a century after political colonialism ended. Various intellectual and political influences helped bring about the change—Marxism and the gospel of social art, the belief that European art was decadent and the explosive effect of Mexican revolutionary art, in which Indianism played a strong part. As a result painters and sculptors as well as writers turned to the Indians—Indian faces, the landscapes of Indian country and Indian folk arts—for material. Probably the best-known single artist in the *indigenista* movement was the Peruvian José Sabogal, who became director of Peru's School of Fine Arts in 1933. There were similar trends in Ecuador and Bolivia, and the painting and sculpture of the Andean region have tended to be dominated by stocky Indian bodies and anguished Indian faces.

There was also a growing recognition of the excellence of the works of art produced by the Indians themselves—both the products of the ancient cultures and the work of present-day Indians. Collecting pre-Columbian artifacts for their esthetic as well as their archeological value became a vogue in the 1930s. *Huaqueros,* or grave robbers, became busy men in Peru and Ecuador—and so did those artisans who could manufacture reasonable facsimiles of Chimu pottery and Paracas textiles. Much more legitimate and important, the really magnificent work still being done by certain Indians in ceramics, wood sculpture and textiles is beginning to be widely appreciated. With the aid of such sympathetic entrepreneurs as Olga Fisch in Quito, Ecuador, the contemporary folk arts of the Indians are finding their way into distinguished collections in North America and Europe.

Indianism in the arts reached the peak of its influence in the 1930s. Inevitably there was a reaction away from it, and currently the great majority of artists in the four Andean countries are members of the vast international school of Abstract Expressionism, although some of the best, such as Fernando de Szyszlo of Peru, find inspiration in the intricate designs of pre-Columbian art. But, as Szyszlo says, "I try to use my Peruvian tradition as the tools for a contemporary language." Oswaldo Guayasamín of Ecuador, who probably has as wide an international reputation as any painter in the four countries, is an almost full-blooded Indian and is proud of it. His painting, however, is more universal than Indian. Bolivian painter Jorge Carrasco occasionally has hints of the stark Altiplano landscape in his paintings, but for the most part they are wholly abstract. His cousin, the sculptress Marina Núñez del Prado, works in native Andean stone and Bolivian hardwoods and uses mountains, condors and Indian women as models, but she refines them to graceful, simple, abstract shapes.

Chile took no part in the arguments for and against Indianism. Chilean writers and artists are more sophisticated and international than those of the other Andean countries. Of the best-known contemporary Chilean painters—Roberto Matta, Enrique Zañartu, Nemesio Antúnez and Ernesto Barreda— the first two live and work in Paris, and none of them do paintings of Indian subjects.

Despite the Chileans' reputation as a pragmatic people and as compulsive historians ("No part of Chile's past has been left unstudied, no document in its archives unpublished or unexplained," wrote a Spanish critic), their greatest literary achievement has been in the lyric poetry of Gabriela Mistral and Pablo Neruda. Both are revered in all parts of the world, although Neruda's commitment to the political Left sometimes makes him, if not his poetry, a subject of controversy.

The habit of controversy, usually political, which seems to pervade all aspects of intellectual life in the Andean nations, is nowhere more apparent than in the universities. Politically motivated student demonstrations are common and frequently violent. One of the early steps taken by the military junta that seized the Government of Ecuador in 1963 was to curb what it considered subversive activity among students and faculty of the Central University of Ecuador. The students were forbidden to stage their traditional annual demonstration protesting against the Protocol of Rio de Janeiro, an agreement signed in 1942 ceding a large part of Ecuador's national territory to the hated Peruvians. The junta gave as its reason the supposed involvement of "discontented politicians and Communists" in the planned demonstration.

The students demonstrated despite the ban. Some were arrested; others were driven back to the university by mounted police, armed soldiers and tear-gas squads. University professors who marched on the national palace to protest the arrest of the students were given the same rough treatment. The students barricaded themselves in the university and proclaimed it "free territory and the general headquarters of those who are ready to fight for liberation of the country." After a stormy siege the police and soldiers broke the students' resistance and hauled them off by truckloads to prison. Two months later, "having taken steps for its orderly progress"—which

---

VERSES BY A LEADING ANDEAN POET

Pablo Neruda, Chile's greatest living poet, writes many political verses, but his fame rests on lyrics such as this, from "The Sea Gulls of Antofagasta":

Above the cruel mountains of mineral
Behind my ship,
I saw man and love arise
In a farewell flight of sea gulls.
Triangular and gray
They took form
Above the disappearing Antofagasta,
And in their flight, they cut
Fugitive rectangles.
Light and geometry criss-crossed
Immoveable, they came nearer.
They seemed to rise in their own foam
And suddenly they became lines of salt,
Eyes of the sky or eyebrows above the snow.

included dismissal of professors, expulsion of students and dissolution of the student federation—the junta permitted the university to reopen, but with its previous autonomy destroyed.

"University autonomy" is a key phrase in the intellectual life of the Andean nations. The principal universities date back to the 16th and 17th Centuries (San Marcos in Lima, founded in 1551, was the first university on the continent). They were at first Catholic, and although they produced some brilliant men they were narrow in academic scope and enrollment was limited. After independence the universities became public institutions, broader in both curricula and enrollment, but they were still rigidly controlled, this time by the various Governments.

Recognition of the universities' need for autonomy developed into the University Reform Movement which originated at the University of Córdoba in Argentina in 1918 and quickly spread to Peru, Chile, Ecuador and the rest of Spanish America. The reform movement was aimed at democratizing and modernizing the old institutions. Government of the universities was to be in the hands of faculty and students. The universities were to be freed from class and racial prejudice and put within the reach of the needy. Faculty members' teaching effectiveness was to be subject to review. There were to be more seminars and open discussions and fewer lectures.

THE reform movement produced a great deal of both intellectual and political ferment. Where the universities earlier had reflected the political temper of the country, national politics now began to reflect agitation within the universities. Political activity in the universities sometimes seemed to overshadow academic pursuits. Student demonstrations of all sorts, including riots and hunger strikes, became commonplace. Occasionally they have become international incidents. It was students at the University of San Marcos in Lima who stoned U.S. Vice President Richard Nixon in 1958. In times of national unrest mounted police and high-pressure water trucks are always found in the vicinity of the universities, ready for violence. At a provincial university in Peru students who were allegedly Communist-led recently broke up classes, seized the university, locked the doors, went on a hunger strike and then announced that order would not be restored until the "dictatorial" rector agreed to the appointment of a known Communist to the faculty.

A North American exchange student at the University of San Marcos watched with amazement the 1964 election campaigns staged by candidates for offices in the student government. The student candidates ran on tickets with the same names and principles as the national political parties. Their campaigns were both encouraged and financially aided by the national parties. Debates were on national or international issues, not academic ones. Student candidates ranged in age from 25 to 40, and some appeared to be making careers out of being students. Campaign rallies often ended in bloody fights. The gardens in the university patios were trampled underfoot; age-smooth walls were defaced with posters. Seminars turned into heated political wrangles. Schedules of classes were disrupted or abandoned.

THE exchange student wrote a polite letter to a Lima newspaper, commenting on how strange these things seemed. The newspaper replied with an editorial: ". . . it is so. . . . we come to the University to find everything for the realization of our ideals and find nothing more than chaos . . . an entanglement of Byzantine discussion like a parody of our parliamentary or forensic futility . . . we desired ardently that the Peruvian university should fulfill its academic function without partisan, nonacademic interference. . . . The vices which sicken our university life cannot be understood by someone who has not suffered them. . . . These peripheral vices are nothing more than revealing signs of grave syndromes in the economic and social order. . . ."

The "revealing signs of grave syndromes" that bothered the writer of the editorial are not confined to the universities. They are found in all areas of cultural and creative effort in the Andean countries. The writers who pour their passion into political tracts instead of poems, like the students who abandon their studies to demonstrate, are reacting to their nations' "grave syndromes" of political, social and economic disorder. But these efforts to find answers and to achieve some measure of order are vigorous in the extreme, and hopefully will produce not only change but also progress.

Painters and writers carry on a lively discussion of Peru's difficulties in the Lima home of Señora Montoya, a patron of the arts.

Intellectuals and Students Involved in Politics

Virtually all of the artists and writers in the Andean nations are what French intellectuals call *"engagé,"* that is, they are passionately engaged not only with the various problems of their crafts but also with politics and justice. Especially since the 1930s, when all the Andean countries faced economic chaos and political upheaval, poets, novelists and painters have vigorously espoused political causes and have made their books and paintings pleas for social reforms. Many have found their answers on the Left; almost all have pleaded the cause of the Indians. Following their lead, students have rushed into the political arena, demonstrating and often rioting to dramatize their solutions to their nations' nagging problems.

CREATIVE ARTISTS *have stirred both the imagination and the conscience of their peoples*

MASTERFUL POET, Chile's Pablo Neruda writes brilliant, didactic poems influenced by Marxism. Neruda wrote personal lyrics until he became politically aroused by Spain's Civil War.

INDIAN PAINTER, Oswaldo Guayasamín stands in front of a recent work in his Quito studio. He has done a cycle of 100 paintings which tell the story of his native Ecuador.

RESPECTED WRITER, Peru's Ciro Alegría publishes novels that champion the Indian. An early member of the APRA party, he spent several years in exile for his political views.

REVERED POETESS, Gabriela Mistral of Chile *(below)* is considered one of the modern era's finest writers. Her passionate, lyric poems won her the Nobel Prize in 1945. She died in 1957.

VIGOROUS NOVELIST, José María Arguedas *(below)* writes of the poor of his native Peru with a sober lyricism. His works protest against the squalor in which many Peruvians must live.

QUIET COURTYARD at Lima's San Marcos university is nonetheless the spot where a board announces student rallies, in this case a meeting in memory of the poet García Lorca.

STUDENT REVOLUTIONARIES at the University of San Andrés in La Paz, Bolivia *(below)*, discuss the part they played in the overthrow of President Paz Estenssoro's Government.

UNIVERSITY DEMONSTRATORS stand with a banner on the steps of the cathedral in Quito, Ecuador, in January 1965 during their annual "Silent March for National Dignity"

protesting a cession of Ecuadorian territory to Peru, which took place in 1942. The march was far from silent as the students yelled slogans assailing Ecuador's ruling military junta and "Yankee imperialism." Afterward some of the marchers attacked the Government Palace with rocks and Molotov cocktails, and the final toll was five injured and 14 arrested.

Bolivian Indians and mestizos, guarded by bayonet-wielding troops, hear a speech by General Barrientos shortly after he had seized power in

1964. *To curry favor with the Indians, Barrientos spoke in Quechua.*

10

Agitation from the Center

THE whole Andean region is an emerging world —politically, economically, socially. Its past is one of repression, disappointment and, frequently, disaster. The conquistadors all came to dismal ends in this promising land and so did the liberators three centuries later. Almost a century and a half after the overthrow of Spanish rule the four Andean nations are deeply engaged in a struggle to become modern, functioning democracies. New political parties, alliances and philosophies are taking shape. The old rigidities of social and economic order are crumbling. The oligarchies that have controlled the countries from the time of the conquest are still powerful, but their control is now greatly diminished (and in the case of Bolivia has almost disappeared). Sons of oligarchs are active in political parties and social movements that would have been anathema to their forebears. White- and blue-collar classes have emerged and are proving their political potency and social mobility.

Even the Indians, who make up a large proportion of the population in Peru, Ecuador and Bolivia, are

145

beginning to disprove the old view of them as an inert human mass, silent, withdrawn and passive. Many Indians, it is true, remain primitive, living in squalor, doomed to short lives for lack of food and sanitation. Few of them are economically effective; most produce just enough to feed and clothe themselves. As a people they have, as Peruvian novelist Ciro Alegría wrote, "died a death four centuries long and . . . suffered all the sorrows that time holds." But they have begun to change. In Bolivia, where the 1952 revolution made them voters and landowners, the Indians are becoming 20th Century people, alert, ambitious and conscious of their strength. In Peru, where they have taken over large tracts of land by force, thousands of Indians have demonstrated a readiness to die for any cause that gives them even a vague hope for the future.

THE problems the four Andean nations face are large and complicated. Most basic of these problems concerns the ownership and use of the land. Each of the four countries has a predominantly agricultural society, and each has in recent years adopted some sort of agrarian reform law in the multiple interest of social justice, reducing potentially revolutionary pressures and producing more food for growing populations. Bolivia in 1953 virtually eliminated large holdings and distributed the expropriated land among the peasants. Nine years later Chile adopted an agrarian reform law, but in its first two years of operation it had benefited fewer than 2,000 families. Laws for the expropriation and distribution of land have since been adopted by Peru and Ecuador, but there is a grave question whether such measures have been taken soon enough and whether there is enough land to go around.

Meanwhile the populations of the four Andean nations are increasing at unprecedented rates. There is a population drift from rural to urban areas, and this has caused a startling growth in the shantytowns that huddle in and around the cities. In some cases life is better in the shantytowns than it was in the country, but there is little hope for the future. There is, instead, a potential for unrest. In Santiago, the capital of Chile, one of the new slums, called La Victoria, has become an autonomous Communist village, self-governed and fiercely independent.

Greater industrialization could provide jobs for the poverty-stricken people of the shantytowns and hasten their integration into the societies of the four countries. But industrialization requires a mass market, capital and a broadly based economy. A majority of Andean peoples—urban or rural—still live on a subsistence level and provide almost no market for manufactured goods. There is little generation of capital and no surplus of cash beyond that required for the bare necessities. Further, three of the four countries continue to depend on one or two exportable products—Chile depends on copper and nitrates, Bolivia on tin and Ecuador on bananas. Such dependence makes them peculiarly susceptible to phenomena over which they have no control. A slight fluctuation in the world price of copper can produce a financial disaster; a bad crop of bananas can lead to political chaos.

Various cures have been tried. There have been attempts to create a mass market, develop capital and diversify exports. Unfortunately the attempts frequently have been haphazard, the result of improvisation rather than rational planning. The characteristic pattern in most of the Andean countries (Chile, as in many other things, is an exception) throughout the 19th Century and into the 20th was rule by *caudillos*, strongmen who rose to power either through eminence as military men or persuasiveness as demagogues. Either way, the base of the strongman's power was not so much a systematic program as it was the strength of his personality or the hardness of his fist. Action was taken in response to crises rather than according to plan, and taken in the interest of the *caudillo* and the ruling classes. Some observers feel that the attraction Marxism has had in these and other Latin American countries is due simply to the fact that it seems to offer a plan, a complete ideology, a plausible answer to all problems.

THE first two notable exceptions in the Andean countries to this pattern of political, social and economic improvisation occurred in Chile and Peru at approximately the same time—the early 1920s. Both Arturo Alessandri in his first term as President of Chile (1920-1924) and the Alianza Popular Revolucionaria Americana (APRA) party in Peru seemed to offer specific answers to specific problems.

Chile was socially more advanced and politically more sophisticated than its Andean neighbors, but it remained for Alessandri to take note of (and make political use of) the rapidly growing middle and working classes. The APRA movement in Peru, founded and led by Víctor Raúl Haya de la Torre, similarly linked the middle and working classes, getting leadership from one and political strength from the other. APRA originally had many links with Marxism, but there were also many important differences. Latin America's rural proletariat, Haya thought, could not carry on the revolutionary struggle alone, as an industrialized European proletariat might; instead, the cooperation of the middle class was needed.

THERE were and are many middle-class characteristics in the APRA program. An almost puritanical morality was demanded of the party's members. There was to be no drinking, no smoking, no chewing of coca, no card playing and no sexual licentiousness. The production of wholesome foods that Peruvians needed—meat, grain for bread and dairy products—should have priority over the production of export goods. And although it was at times involved in violence APRA urged its members not to rely on violence as a weapon.

Thus APRA, a mass party, mobilized illiterate Indians in the highlands and industrial workers in the cities along the coast and, in addition, gave voice—just as had the regime of Arturo Alessandri in Chile—to the discontents and hopes of a rising middle class in Latin America. With such a broadly based alliance APRA has constituted a formidable barrier to Communism in Peru and is an expression of the nationalistic, non-Communist Left that is, more and more, guiding the destinies not only of the Andean countries but of much of Latin America.

Such expressions of nationalism are characteristic of the new, progressive, middle-class doctrines. They reflect a feeling that Governmental and economic formulas developed by other nations, whether the United States or Russia, cannot be transplanted successfully. There are other areas of agreement: that existing political and social structures need to be reformed; that the individual countries need economic

development and that the Government should intervene in such development, even if nationalization of industry and resources is required; and that changes should come about by democratic means.

The rise of the revolution-minded middle class is typified, in different ways, by three outstanding political figures of the Andean countries: Víctor Paz Estenssoro, who played the leading role in the Bolivian National Revolution; Fernando Belaúnde Terry, who became President of Peru in 1963; and Eduardo Frei, who was elected to the presidency of Chile in 1964.

Víctor Paz Estenssoro boasted that the Bolivian revolution of 1952 was the work of "middle-class intellectuals" who had thought out Bolivia's problems. "They were well aware of and had studied the many existing political doctrines," he has said. "They did not search for a solution in Utopia. Instead they trained their sights inward, thoroughly analyzing the dynamics of Bolivian society. As a result they evolved a pragmatic, genuinely Bolivian train of thought that reflects the aspirations, hopes and interests of the vast majority of the population."

In order to assume the leadership of this "vast majority," Paz, the middle-class intellectual, became a wily politician and an expert manipulator of the sentiments of the *campesinos*, who supported him with fierce loyalty. For more than a decade he was the dominant figure of the Bolivian revolution, and although he was in time overthrown he was the embodiment of the new-style revolutionists who are doing much to change the character of the Andean nations. Bolivia, no less than its neighbors, Paz feels, is "engaged in a race against time, because we need to satisfy dire needs to save the country from explosive situations." The unspoken alternative is a Communist take-over.

FERNANDO BELAUNDE TERRY, an architect, was elected President of Peru pledged to "revolutionary reform of national structures." In this and many other ways he represents, just as Paz in Bolivia and Frei in Chile, the new political activism and determination of labor and of the growing middle class. Early in his political career he flirted with APRA, and although APRA has actively opposed him, there are strong similarities between the program of APRA and that of Belaúnde's Acción Popular party. This program attracted support from widely different sources—the middle class, labor, rural elements in southern and eastern Peru (Belaúnde campaigned vigorously among the Indians), Leftist intellectuals, Christian Democrats, many university students and liberal-minded members of the oligarchy. Even military officers supported him, apparently because they preferred Belaúnde to Víctor Raúl Haya de la Torre, veteran leader of APRA, who opposed Belaúnde in the 1963 election.

WITH the support of such diverse elements Belaúnde, as President, undertook an energetic and progressive program. He pressed for an agrarian reform law which, although the product of much compromise, will alter Peru's archaic system of land ownership and will place many Indians on land of their own. He pushed low-cost housing, extended universal free education through the university level, and set up a nonpolitical organization, Cooperación Popular, to speed road building, school construction and sanitation projects in the interior of the country. His great dream of a highway along the eastern approaches of the Andes may someday open up to development a potentially rich but little-used region that constitutes almost two thirds of Peru's land area.

Unlike the revolution in Bolivia, which came about by a sudden and violent upheaval that obliterated the old order, Peru's political change came as the result of complicated political maneuvering. In each case, however, the political Left united with the middle-class leadership to bring about change.

But in Chile the parties of the far Left, the Socialists and the Communists, both of which have many middle-class members, united in an effort to defeat an even stronger expression of middle-class discontent, the Christian Democrats—and failed. In the 1964 Chilean election the Christian Democrats won a presidency for the first time in Latin America, and in so doing became a force to reckon with in the hemisphere. Christian Democrats form an important part of the coalition with which President Belaúnde governs Peru, and are active in Bolivia. After the congressional election of March 1965 Frei's Christian Democrats held 82 seats in the Chamber of Deputies, making it the first party to have an absolute majority in more than 100 years.

The Christian Democrats in Chile are in some ways almost as far to the left as their Socialist-Communist opponents. They propose a revolution, but a "revolution with freedom." The movement had its beginnings in the 1930s, when Frei and other Catholic students began to drift away from the old Conservative Party. Frei, the son of a Swiss immigrant, while still a student, organized seminars on Chile's social problems. Somewhat later he studied in Paris under Jacques Maritain, principal theorist of the Christian Democratic movement, and he was also influenced by the social encyclicals of Popes Leo XIII and Pius XI (and later by those of Pope John XXIII).

Frei and his colleagues opposed a law banning the Communist Party in Chile in 1948, preferring to combat Marxism on ideological grounds. They considered themselves just as revolutionary as the Marxists in so far as they favored "profound structural changes" in Chilean society, but they proposed to make them by peaceful, legal means. "Our object," Frei has said, "is to serve the people and to make a government that will take decisive action to raise the country's moral and material condition, not in a paternalistic sense but in a way to promote the human values of our own people." He has gone on to assert that the "Marxist-Leninist formula could be useful for people so underdeveloped that they do not know liberty or have had no democratic experience. But here, where we have democracy, where there are germs of economic development, there is no need to regiment the life of the nation under the iron fist of a dictatorship."

REVOLUTIONARY forces—philosophical in Chile, violent in Bolivia, evolving in Peru and suppressed but present in Ecuador—are at work in all of the Andean countries. The speed at which these forces work, attacking the age-old problems imposed by a tradition of repression and a physical environment that has always challenged man's courage and ingenuity, is a matter of concern not only to the Andean republics themselves but to the entire Free World. The pressures are great and change is inevitable; only the extent and the ultimate character of the change remain to be seen.

A market-day crowd fills a narrow street in Quito, which, although a centuries-old center of Andean culture, remains a busy city.

CROWDING INTO CITIES that are not yet equipped to provide for them . . .

On the Peruvian shore of Lake Titicaca a group of Aymara Indians twirls through a dance to the music of flutes and drums. The site of

... or living still at the measured pace of old traditions, the Andean people are slowly

an ancient culture called the Tiahuanaco, the lake's relatively fertile shores still support more Indians than do the surrounding highlands.

responding to the tempo of an age that may bring relief to their long-continued poverty

Appendix

HISTORICAL DATES

B.C.

c.9000 Nomadic hunters arrive in Peru

c.8000-1200 Hunting communities begin to fish and to use plants for food. Permanent farming and fishing communities develop

c.1200 Later arrivals introduce pottery and new types of dwellings

c.1000 B.C.-900 A.D. The unification of Peru begins with the diffusion of Chavín art and religion. Chavín influence declines; other distinct regional cultures develop

A.D.

c.900 A gradual reunification of the various Indian groups takes place; Tiahuanaco culture diffuses through the central Andes

1100-1438 Strong regional governments are re-established; beginnings of Inca culture in highlands

1438-1527 Incas conquer neighboring peoples and establish a military empire, building great cities and a vast road network. Disruption sets in with division of empire after the death of the Inca Huayna Capac in 1527

1513 Vasco Núñez de Balboa discovers the Pacific

1524-1528 Francisco Pizarro heads two exploratory expeditions to the coast of Ecuador and Peru. In 1529 the Spanish Crown signs *capitulación* giving Pizarro the right of discovery and conquest in the province of Peru. Pizarro recruits four of his brothers for his third expedition

1532-1534 Pizarro marches on the Inca Atahuallpa's headquarters at Cajamarca. Atahuallpa is executed. Pizarro takes Cuzco, and his partner Diego de Almagro secures Quito

1535-1537 Pizarro founds Lima. Almagro marches to take possession of Chile. On his return he captures Cuzco. Strife between Almagro and the Pizarros leads to civil war

1538-1541 Battle of Las Salinas won by the Pizarros, who execute Almagro. Almagro's son rallies followers to oppose the Pizarros; Francisco Pizarro and his half brother Francisco Martín de Alcántara are assassinated

1540 Pedro de Valdivia begins the conquest of Chile. He founds the city of Santiago in 1541, but is killed battling Araucanian Indians in 1553

1542-1548 Civil war and rebellion continue. Young Almagro rebels against the Spanish envoy but is defeated and executed. Gonzalo Pizarro then leads a rebellion against Viceroy Blasco Núñez Vela, who arrives from Spain. Gonzalo kills the Viceroy but is in turn executed by a third envoy from Spain

1545 Great silver mines of Potosí are discovered

1551 The University of San Marcos, the first university established in South America, is founded in Lima

1570 Inquisition established in Peru

1571 Last uprising of the Incas under Tupac Amaru is crushed

1661-1824 Indians in Bolivia periodically rebel against Spanish authority. They besiege La Paz for nine months in 1781

1806 Francisco de Miranda makes a futile attempt to liberate Venezuela from Spain

1809 An unsuccessful revolt against Spanish rule takes place in Bolivia

1810 Wars of independence begin with revolt in Venezuela

1817-1818 José de San Martín and Bernardo O'Higgins defeat the Spanish at Chacabuco and Maipú, the decisive battles for Chilean independence

1819 Simón Bolívar frees Colombia at battle of Boyacá

1821 San Martín takes Lima and declares Peru independent of Spain

1822 Bolívar and San Martín meet at Guayaquil. Battle of Pichincha leads to Ecuador's independence from Spain

1824 Antonio José de Sucre defeats the Spanish at Ayacucho in the last decisive battle for South American independence

1825-1826 Last royalist forces are defeated by Sucre at Tumusla, Bolivia. Bolivia declares its independence as a nation, names itself for Bolívar and elects Sucre first President. Sucre is exiled in 1828

1836-1839 Confederation of Peru and Bolivia engineered by Bolivian President Andrés Santa Cruz. Chile declares war and breaks up the confederation

1845-1867 Peruvian politics dominated by Ramón Castilla

1861-1875 Gabriel García Moreno, a Catholic Conservative, leads Ecuador from 30 years of chaos into a period of development

1872 Civilista Party elects Manuel Pardo first civilian President of Peru

1879-1883 War of the Pacific. Chile defeats Peru and Bolivia and gains control of the nitrates and silver in the Atacama Desert

1895-1916 Era of reform in Ecuador under Presidents Eloy Alfaro and Leonidas Plaza

1899 Discovery of tin by the "tin baron," Simón I. Patiño, signals the beginning of vast tin-mining operations in Bolivia

1903 Bolivia loses the Acre region to Brazil

1920-1930 Foreign capital increases its stake in Bolivian oil and tin

1924 Arturo Alessandri, President of Chile, begins a broad program of social reforms. Víctor Raúl Haya de la Torre founds APRA party in Peru

1932-1935 Bolivia loses the Chaco War with Paraguay

1936-1950 Bolivian defeat in the Chaco War produces a period of general unrest. President Germán Busch pushes through some reforms but his program comes to an abrupt end with his death. President Gualberto Villarroel is murdered, and various political leaders are exiled. The reform-minded MNR party is born

1948-1952 President Galo Plaza Lasso of Ecuador achieves stability and economic reform

1951 The MNR party wins Bolivian presidential election but is prevented by the military from taking power

1952 The MNR revolts and assumes control of the Bolivian Government, making Víctor Paz Estenssoro President

1952-1964 Under the MNR-controlled Government, Bolivia undergoes one of the most sweeping revolutions in all of Latin America

1960 Severe earthquake takes 4,000 lives in Chile

1963 Military junta takes control of Ecuador

1964 Eduardo Frei, a Christian Democrat, wins presidency of Chile. Military coup exiles Bolivian President Paz and puts Air Force General René Barrientos at head of Government

FOR FURTHER READING

CHAPTER 1: THE MOUNTAIN WORLD

Carlson, Fred A., *Geography of Latin America*. Prentice-Hall, 1943.

Davies, Howell, ed., *The South American Handbook, 1965*. Rand McNally, 1965.

Dozer, Donald Marquand, *Latin America*. McGraw-Hill, 1962.

Herring, Hubert, *A History of Latin America*. Alfred A. Knopf, 1962.

Linke, Lilo, *Andean Adventure*. Hutchinson, Ltd., London, 1945.

Rippy, J. Fred, *Latin America*. University of Michigan Press, 1958.

Sitwell, Sacheverell, *Golden Wall and Mirador; Travels and Observations in Peru*. World Publishing Company, 1961.

Subercaseaux, Benjamín, *Chile, A Geographic Extravaganza*. Macmillan, 1943.

CHAPTER 2: THE INCA EMPIRE

Baudin, Louis, *A Socialist Empire: The Incas of Peru*. D. Van Nostrand, 1961.

Bennett, Wendell C., and Junius B. Bird, *Andean Culture History*. The Natural History Press, 1964.

Bingham, Hiram, *Lost City of the Incas*. Atheneum, 1963.

Bushnell, G.H.S., *Peru; Ancient Peoples and Places*. Frederick A. Praeger, 1963.

Flornoy, Bertrand, *The World of the Inca*. Doubleday Anchor Books, 1958.

Gheerbrant, Alain, ed., *The Incas; The Royal Commentaries of the Inca, Garcilaso de la Vega*. The Orion Press, 1963.

Hyams, Edward, and George Ordish, *The Last of the Incas*. Simon and Schuster, 1963.

Markham, Clements R., *Incas of Peru*. E. P. Dutton, 1910.

Mason, J. Alden, *The Ancient Civilizations of Peru*. Penguin Books, 1964.

Steward, Julian H., ed., *Handbook of South American Indians*, Vol. II. U.S. Government Printing Office, 1946.

Steward, Julian H., and Louis C. Faron, *Native Peoples of South America*. McGraw-Hill, 1959.

Von Hagen, Victor Wolfgang, ed., *The Incas of Pedro de Cieza de León*. University of Oklahoma Press, 1959.

CHAPTER 3: THE SPANISH CONQUEST

Bourne, Edward Gaylord, *Spain in America, 1450-1580*. Barnes & Noble, 1962.

Haring, C. H., *The Spanish Empire in America*. Oxford University Press, 1947.

Helps, Arthur, *Spanish Conquest in America*. 4 vols. John Lane Co., 1900-1904.

Madariaga, Salvador de, *The Fall of the Spanish American Empire*. Macmillan, 1948. *The Rise of the Spanish American Empire*. Macmillan, 1947.

Means, Philip A., *Fall of the Inca Empire, and the Spanish Rule in Peru, 1530-1780*. Charles Scribner's Sons, 1932.

Merriman, Roger Bigelow, *The Rise of the Spanish Empire in the Old World and in the New*. 4 vols. Macmillan, 1936.

Prescott, William H., *History of the Conquest of Mexico and History of the Conquest of Peru*. Modern Library, 1936.

CHAPTER 4: THE LIBERATION

Beals, Carleton, *Eagles of the Andes*. Chilton Books, 1963.

Harrison, Margaret H., *Captain of the Andes; The Life of Don José de San Martín*. Richard R. Smith, 1943.

Madariaga, Salvador de, *Bolivar*. Pellegrini & Cudahy, 1952.

Masur, Gerhard, *Simon Bolivar*. University of New Mexico Press, 1948.

Pendle, George, *A History of Latin America*. Penguin Books, 1963.

Robertson, William Spence, *Rise of the Spanish-American Republics As Told in the Lives of Their Liberators*. Collier Books, 1961.

CHAPTER 5: PERU AND THE INDIAN

Ford, Thomas R., *Man and Land in Peru*. University of Florida Press, 1962.

Kantor, Harry, *Ideology and Program of the Peruvian Aprista Movement*. University of California Press, 1953.

Owens, R. J., *Peru*. Oxford University Press, 1963.

CHAPTER 6: ECUADOR

Bemelmans, Ludwig, *The Donkey Inside*. E. P. Dutton, 1964.

Blanksten, George I., *Ecuador: Constitutions and Caudillos*. University of California Press, 1951.

Franklin, Albert B., *Ecuador: Portrait of a People*. Doubleday Doran, 1943.

Linke, Lilo, *Ecuador: Country of Contrasts*. Oxford University Press, 1960.

CHAPTER 7: BOLIVIA

Alexander, Robert J., *The Bolivian National Revolution*. Rutgers University Press, 1958.

La Barre, Weston, "The Aymara Indians of the Lake Titicaca Plateau, Bolivia." *American Anthropologist*, Vol. 50, January 1948.

Osborne, Harold, *Bolivia: A Land Divided*. Oxford University Press, 1964. *Indians of the Andes*. Harvard University Press, 1952.

CHAPTER 8: CHILE

Bowers, Claude G., *Chile Through Embassy Windows: 1939-1953*. Simon and Schuster, 1958.

Clissold, Stephen, *Chilean Scrapbook*. The Cresset Press, 1952.

Fergusson, Erne, *Chile*. Alfred A. Knopf, 1943.

Galdames, Luis, *A History of Chile*. University of North Carolina Press, 1941.

Graham, R. B. Cunninghame, *Pedro de Valdivia*. Harper & Brothers, 1927.

Kirkpatrick, F. A., *Latin America; A Brief History*. Macmillan, 1939.

McBride, George McCutchen, *Chile: Land and Society*. American Geographical Society, 1936.

Markham, Clements R., *The War Between Peru and Chile, 1879-1882*. Sampson Low, Marston and Company, Ltd., 1882.

Pendle, George, *The Land and People of Chile*. Macmillan, 1964.

CHAPTER 9: THE ARTS

Anderson Imbert, Enrique, *Spanish-American Literature; A History*. Wayne State University Press, 1963.

Flakoll, Darwin J., and Claribel Alegría, *New Voices of Hispanic America; An Anthology*. Beacon Press, 1962.

Hanke, Lewis, *South America*. D. Van Nostrand, 1959.

Henríquez-Ureña, Pedro, *Literary Currents in Hispanic America*. Harvard University Press, 1945.

Isherwood, Christopher, *The Condor and the Cows*. Random House, 1949.

Jones, Willis Knapp, ed., *Spanish-American Literature in Translation Since 1888*. Frederick Ungar, 1963.

Kelemen, Pál, *Baroque and Rococo in Latin America*. Macmillan, 1951.

Music of Latin America. Pan American Union, 1953.

Picón-Salas, Mariano, *A Cultural History of Spanish America From Conquest to Independence*. University of California Press, 1963.

Slonimsky, Nicolas, *Music of Latin America*. Thomas Y. Crowell Company, 1945.

Wethey, H. E., *Colonial Architecture and Sculpture in Peru*. Harvard University Press, 1949.

CHAPTER 10: PROMISES AND PROBLEMS

Alexander, Robert J., *Today's Latin America*. Anchor Books, 1962.

Council on Foreign Relations, *Social Change in Latin America Today*. Harper & Brothers, 1960.

Maier, Joseph, and Richard W. Weatherhead, eds., *Politics of Change in Latin America*. Frederick A. Praeger, 1964.

Needler, Martin C., ed., *Political Systems of Latin America*. D. Van Nostrand, 1964.

Powelson, John P., *Latin America: Today's Economic and Social Revolution*. McGraw-Hill, 1964.

FAMOUS ANDEAN CULTURAL FIGURES AND THEIR PRINCIPAL WORKS

Cieza de León, Pedro de	1520-1560	Peruvian historian born in Spain. He arrived with the conquistadors, traveled throughout the Inca Empire and wrote an account of Inca life and history: *Crónica del Perú*
Ercilla y Zúñiga, Alonso de	1534-1594	Chilean poet born in Spain. A soldier, he was sent to Chile in 1554 to help suppress the Araucanian Indians. Inspired by their heroic fight, he wrote, on the battlefield, an epic poem: *La Araucana*
Garcilaso Inca de la Vega	1539-1616	Peruvian historian. Son of an Inca Princess and a conquistador, he observed the effects of the conquest firsthand, interviewed his relatives on Inca history and wrote a colorful account of the Inca past: *The Royal Commentaries*
Olmedo, José Joaquín de	1780-1847	Ecuadorian poet. Wrote stirring odes inspired by national events and heroes: *La Victoria de Junín;* "*Canto a Bolívar*"; *Al general Flores, vencedor en Miñarica*
Blest Gana, Alberto	1830-1920	Chilean novelist. One of the first realists, he is considered the father of the Chilean novel: *Los transplantados*
Vicuña Mackenna, Benjamín	1831-1886	Chilean historian, revolutionist, journalist, politician, diplomat and brilliant writer of history: *El ostracismo del general D. Bernardo O'Higgins, Historia de Valparaíso*
Montalvo, Juan	1832-1889	Ecuadorian prose writer who protested against the evils of society: *Siete tratados*
Palma, Ricardo	1833-1919	Peruvian writer. Historical anecdotes and folk tales about Lima from the time of the Incas to the early 20th Century: *Tradiciones peruanas*
González Prada, Manuel	1848-1918	Peruvian critic. Polemic prose, criticism and social philosophy: *Grafitos*
Matto de Turner, Clorinda	1854-1909	Peruvian novelist. Her dramatic and romantic novel of an Indian couple, *Aves sin nido*, describes the plight of the Andean Indians
Lillo, Baldomero	1867-1923	Chilean short-story writer who told of hardship in the coal mines in the manner of the French naturalists: *Sub Sole, Sub Terra, Relatos populares*
Jaimes Freyre, Ricardo	1868-1933	Bolivian poet. Wrote on poetical theory: *Revista Americana, Castalia barbara*
Arguedas, Alcides	1879-1946	Bolivian novelist. His *Raza de bronce* tells of the treatment of Indians by Creole landlords and their mestizo servants. *Vida criolla* is a novel of city life
Tamayo, Franz	1880-1956	Bolivian poet who began in the French romantic tradition but later became a Modernist: *Scopas, Epigramas griegos*
Barrios, Eduardo	1884-1963	Chilean novelist and short-story writer: *El niño que enloqueció del amor*
Latorre, Mariano	1886-1955	Chilean novelist who also wrote short stories: *Zurzulita, Ully*
Edwards Bello, Joaquín	1886-	Chilean novelist. Writes of abnormal people. *El roto* describes the underworld of Santiago
Mistral, Gabriela	1889-1957	Chilean poet. Nobel laureate whose great lyrical theme was love: *Desolación, Dolor*
Huidobro, Vicente	1893-1948	Chilean poet who spent much time in Madrid and Paris and was influenced by the French poet Apollinaire: *Poemas árticos, Horizon carré*
Mariátegui, José Carlos	1895-1930	Peruvian essayist. Influential social critic and editor of avant-garde publications: *Siete ensayos de interpretación de la realidad peruana*
Vallejo, César	1895-1938	Peruvian poet of great power who in spite of a tragic life became one of Latin America's outstanding writers. Unjustly imprisoned, he later traveled to Russia and to Paris, where he died in poverty: *Trilce, Poemas humanos*
Rojas, Manuel	1896-	Chilean novelist and short-story writer. Work influenced by the American writers Hemingway and Faulkner: *Hombres del sur, Born Guilty*
Carrión, Benjamín	1898-	Ecuadorian writer of history, biography, poetry, novels and criticism: *Atahuallpa*, a study of the last reigning Inca; *El desencanto de Miguel García*
Brunet, Marta	1901-	Chilean short-story writer and novelist of the Creolist school. She is to Chilean prose what Gabriela Mistral was to verse: *Montaña adentro, María Nadie*
Carrera Andrade, Jorge	1902-	Ecuadorian poet born in a primitive rural town who has traveled widely but still writes excellently of his homeland
Neruda, Pablo	1904-	Chilean poet. One of Latin America's outstanding poets. First a Symbolist (*Crepusculario*), he now uses Surrealist techniques to express his anguish and despair over the social system: *Residence on Earth, España en el corazón*
Icaza, Jorge	1906-	Ecuadorian novelist who writes of the exploitation of the Indian as well as of the problems of the middle class. His works are widely translated: *Huasipungo*
Alegría, Ciro	1909-	Peruvian novelist whose work has been translated widely. He describes the mountains and jungles of his native land and the traditions and folklore of, as well as the injustices suffered by, the Indians: *The Golden Serpent, Broad and Alien Is the World*
Bombal, María Luisa	1910-	Chilean novelist whose works merge reality and dream: *The Shrouded Woman*
Arguedas, José María	1913-	Peruvian novelist and short-story writer. Writes of Indians: *Agua*
Ortiz, Adalberto	1914-	Ecuadorian poet, teacher, painter and novelist. Dominant theme of his novel *Juyungo* is the mixing of the Negro race with Indians and whites. Short stories: *La mala espalda*
Parra, Nicanor	1914-	Chilean poet who has written in many styles, including the Surrealistic: *Anti-Poems*
Alegría, Fernando	1918-	Chilean novelist and essayist. Has written novelistic biographies and a picaresque novel of a Hispanic-American in San Francisco: *My Horse González*
Donoso, José	1924-	Chilean writer. His novel *Coronation* tells of the decline of an upper-class Santiago family and its servants. Short stories: *Veraneo*

Salazar Bondy, Sebastián	1924-	Peruvian writer. Essays, poetry and narrative works. Outstanding for his writing for the theater: *Rodil, No hay isla feliz*
Lafourcade, Enrique	1927-	Chilean writer of poetic prose, short stories and novels: *El príncipe y las ovejas* is reminiscent of medieval tales, *King Ahab's Feast*
Heiremans, Luis Alberto	1928-1964	Chilean writer. Wrote short stories, a novel and several successful plays before his early death. Play: *Blindman's Verses*
Tellier, Jorge	1935-	Chilean poet. Lyrical poetry which expresses a nostalgic and melancholy spirit: *El árbol de la memoria*

PAINTING AND SCULPTURE

Santiago, Miguel de	1655-1706	Ecuadorian painter of the Quito school who never left his native city but whose fame spread to Europe. Probably painted the life of St. Augustine for Augustinian monastery in Quito
Caspicara (Manuel Chili or Chil)	18th Century	Ecuadorian sculptor of the Quito school. Carved altars and saints: *Our Lady of Sorrows*
González, Juan Francisco	1859-1933	Chilean artist considered the father of modern painting in Chile. His use of bright colors approaches Impressionism
Burchard, Pablo	1873-1964	Chilean painter whose paintings of humble and simple subjects such as flowers or shadows on a wall contain a poetical quality most admired by Chile's younger painters
Sabogal, José	1888-1956	Peruvian painter. Initiator of the Indianism movement. Early paintings were of local, native customs but later work was influenced by the belligerent Indianism of Mexican art: *Women of Ayacucho*
Codesido, Julia	1892-	Peruvian Indianist painter known for the vigor of her brushwork and color as well as for the drama of her themes: *At the Church Door, Landscape, Arequipa*
Vinatea Reynoso, Jorge	1900-1931	Peruvian painter. Indianist whose work was animated by a strong esthetic sense: *Chichería Arequipa*
Berdecio, Roberto	1910-	Bolivian painter whose abstract murals show Mexican influence: *The Cube and the Perspective*
Dávila, Alberto	1912-	Peruvian painter. Has progressed from stylized paintings of people and landscapes to elaborate abstract paintings: *Swamp, Woman of the Sea*
Matta, Roberto	1912-	Chilean painter known in Europe and the Americas. No longer limited by the Surrealism of his youth, his work shows a profound engagement with today's world: *Le Vertige d'Eros*
Garafulic, Lily	1914-	Chilean sculptor of monumental figures in the classical tradition: figures of the Twelve Apostles surrounding the Lourdes basilica in Santiago, *The Sun, The Man*
Colvin, Marta	1915-	Chilean sculptor. Powerful abstract sculptures that owe as much to the Easter Island monuments as to Inca figures: *Towers of Silence, Manutara*
Antúnez, Nemesio	1918-	Chilean painter. Work is remarkable for its passionate individuality. Later works show a preoccupation with the human figure: *La Bestia Cordillera, Women Si.* He now lives in New York
Guayasamín, Oswaldo	1919-	Ecuadorian painter whose powerful works reflect the deep feeling for his land and his people. His great 100-painting work, *Huaycayñan (The Way of Tears)*, is divided into three parts—the Indian, the mestizo and the Negro
Núñez del Prado, Marina	1919-	Bolivian sculptor. Uses native materials for her powerful, often tragic figures inspired by Aymara and Quechua myths: *Espíritu de la montaña, American Indian Dance, Dance of the Condors*
Pacheco, María Luísa	1919-	Bolivian painter. Her abstract paintings show the influence of pre-Columbian Bolivia, such as the ancient culture of Tiahuanaco: *Stoic Figure, Altiplano*. Former newspaperwoman and teacher, she now lives in the U.S.
Zañartu, Enrique	1921-	Chilean painter, brother of Nemesio Antúnez. His work shows a deeply felt personal world: *Beachcomber III, Fog with Claws*
Mallol, Sergio	1922-	Chilean sculptor. Small bronzes and large polished marbles: *Saint Francis, Nude Figure*
Roca Rey, Joaquín	1923-	Peruvian sculptor. Works in aluminum, steel and bronze. Figurative dancers and abstract architectural motifs, statues that flow with elegant grace: *Butterfly Hunter*
Szyszlo, Fernando de	1925-	Peruvian painter who studied in Lima and traveled in Europe. On his return he held first really modern exhibit in Peru, resulting in considerable controversy. His lyrical abstractions reveal a deep interest in ancient Peruvian art: *Cajamarca III A*
Balmes, José	1927-	Chilean painter whose tragic and powerful paintings relate him to his Catalonian ancestors: *Peace, Fusilamientos*
Barreda, Ernesto	1927-	Chilean painter known for his theme of sad, decaying wooden doors and windows. His more recent works show a search for romantic light effects done in temperate tones on roughly textured surfaces: *Façade, Shutters*
Villacís, Aníbal	1927-	Ecuadorian painter who now lives in Spain, turns to pre-Hispanic past for themes: *Precolombino*
Yrarrázaval, Ricardo	1931-	Chilean painter who searches for deep expression and uses rich, subdued colors: *Earth Figure, Sea Figure*
Castro-Cid, Enrique	1937-	Chilean artist. In early work he used fine calligraphic lines on white background. Recently exhibited benign, playful robots to show that technical development imitates life: *Natural Speed, Anthropomorphical II*

Credits

The sources for the illustrations in this book appear below. Credits for pictures from left to right are separated by commas, from top to bottom by dashes.

Cover—Cornell Capa from Magnum

8, 9—Cornell Capa from Magnum

15 through 24—Cornell Capa from Magnum

27—Map by Rafael Palacios

28, 29—Courtesy Travaux et Mémoires de l'Institut d'Ethnologie, Paris

32—Cornell Capa from Magnum

33—Marc and Evelyn Bernheim from Rapho-Guillumette

34, 35—Cornell Capa from Magnum

36—Cornell Capa from Magnum courtesy Dr. Engel of the Julio C. Tello Museum of Paracas, Peru

37—Cornell Capa from Magnum courtesy of the Rafael Larco Herrera Archeological Museum, Lima, Peru, except top and center left Cornell Capa from Magnum courtesy of Señora Montoya, Lima, Peru

38 through 43—Cornell Capa from Magnum

47—Culver Pictures

50, 51—Frank Scherschel, Mike Andrews of Bell, Howarth Ltd. from Black Star—Cornell Capa from Magnum (2)

52, 53—Cornell Capa from Magnum

54, 55—Cornell Capa from Magnum courtesy Don Pedro de Osma, Lima, Peru

56—Cornell Capa from Magnum

59—Map by Rafael Palacios

65 through 71—Cornell Capa from Magnum

72, 73—Forbert from Freelance Photographers Guild

80 through 88—Cornell Capa from Magnum

95 through 100—Cornell Capa from Magnum

103—From the book *Dichos y Hechos del General Melagarejo* by Tomás O'Connor D'Arlach courtesy of Editorial Gisbert y Cia, La Paz, Bolivia

108—Dmitri Kessel, Cornell Capa from Magnum

109 through 118—Cornell Capa from Magnum

125 through 128—Cornell Capa from Magnum

129—Mike Andrews of Bell, Howarth Ltd. from Black Star—Cornell Capa from Magnum

130, 131—Cornell Capa from Magnum except right Sergio Larrain from Magnum

132—Samuel L. Milbank

137—Translated by Willis Knapp Jones, from *Spanish-American Literature in Translation, A Selection of Poetry, Fiction, and Drama Since 1888,* edited by Willis Knapp Jones. Published by Frederick Ungar Publishing Co., New York

139—Cornell Capa from Magnum

140, 141—Sergio Larrain from Magnum, Cornell Capa from Magnum—Baldomero Pestana, Baldomero Pestana—Walter Bennett

142, 143, 144—Cornell Capa from Magnum

149, 150, 151—Cornell Capa from Magnum

ACKNOWLEDGMENTS

The editors are indebted to Robert J. Alexander, Professor of Economics, Rutgers University; and Gregory Rabassa, Associate Professor of Spanish and Portuguese, Columbia University; both of whom read and commented on the text. Valuable assistance was also provided by Jorge Jurado, Tomás A. Loayza, Walter Montenegro and Mario Planet.

Cornell Capa, who took many of the pictures for this book, wishes to express his appreciation to Jorge Bertozzi, John Bratton, Victoriano Chavez, Julio Corbacho, Julio Cornejo, Bruno Frindt, Maximino Oliver, Carlos de la Paz and Luís Perez.

Index

This symbol in front of a page number indicates a photograph or painting of the subject mentioned.

Production staff for Time Incorporated

John L. Hallenbeck (Vice President and Director of Production)

Robert E. Foy, James P. Menton, Caroline Ferri and Robert E. Fraser

Text photocomposed under the direction of

Albert J. Dunn and Arthur J. Dunn

X

Printed by R. R. Donnelley & Sons Company, Crawfordsville, Indiana

and The Safran Printing Company, Detroit, Michigan

Bound by R. R. Donnelley & Sons Company, Crawfordsville, Indiana

Paper by The Mead Corporation, Dayton, Ohio

Cover stock by The Plastic Coating Corporation, Holyoke, Massachusetts

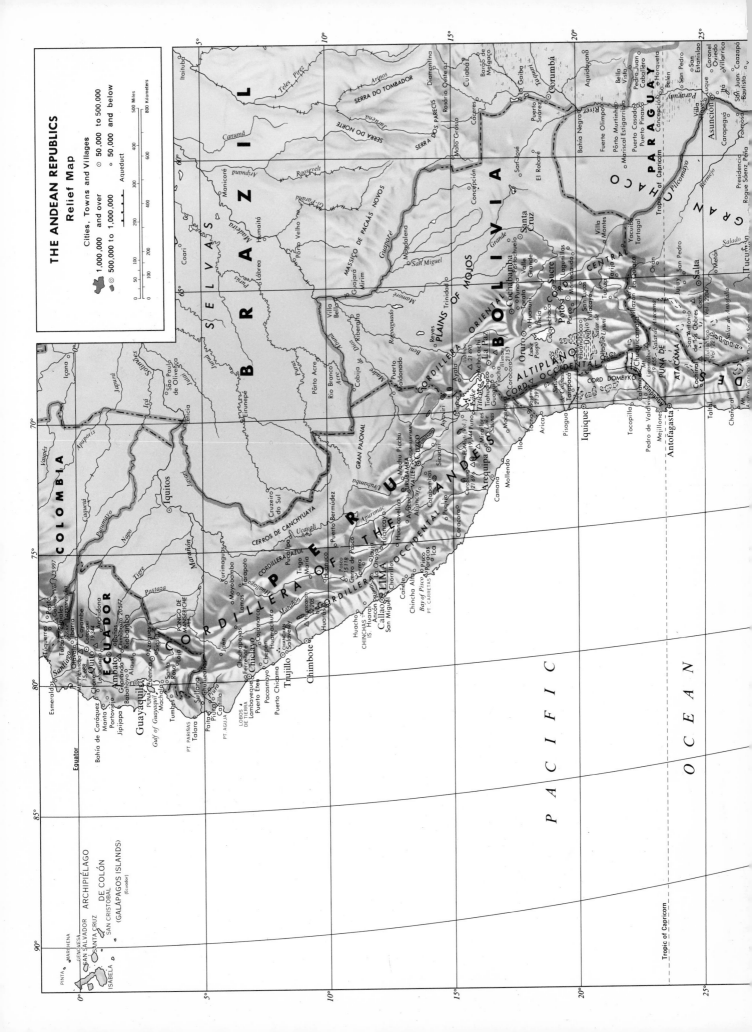

THE ANDEAN REPUBLICS
Relief Map

Cities, Towns and Villages

● 1,000,000 and over   ⊙ 50,000 to 500,000
⊙ 500,000 to 1,000,000   ○ 50,000 and below
⎯⎯⎯ Aqueduct

500 Miles
800 Kilometers